A HUNTER'S JOURNEY

Also by Dan Prusi

Country Boy - Adventures from an Untroubled Childhood
A Hunter's Year

A HUNTER'S JOURNEY

The Education of an Outdoorsman

Dan Prusi

Beaver's Pond Press, Inc.

ISBN 1-931646-71-6

Library of Congress Catalog Number: 2002115610

Cover Photo: Dan Prusi
Design by Dan Prusi and Linda Walters
Typesetting by Linda Walters, Optima Graphics, Appleton, WI

Printed in the United States of America

First Printing: December 2002

06 05 04 03   6 5 4 3 2

Published by Beaver's Pond Press, Inc.
7104 Ohms Lane, Suite 216
Edina, MN 55439-2140
(952) 829-8818
www.beaverspondpress.com

Beaver's Pond Press, Inc.

To Dad
Walter Arne Prusi
1915 - 1971

No matter how young a sportsman is, if he has a healthy mind, he will not long take pleasure in any method of hunting in which somebody else shows the skill and does the work so that his share is only nominal. The minute that sport is carried on on these terms it becomes a sham, and a sham is always detrimental to all who take part in it.

Theodore Roosevelt, **Outdoor Pastimes of an American Hunter**

Contents

Acknowledgements

On the pages of this book, you will read the names of many people to whom I owe very much. When you see such a name, you may safely consider that person to be a trusted friend, and a companion with whom I enjoy spending my precious hours of freedom in the outdoors. I need not list their names on this page, for each knows the esteem, and the gratitude, I feel towards them.

Several members of my extended family made valuable contributions to the actual production of this book. I am indebted to them. Lisa Prusi, Heather Prusi, and my sister, Kathy Tuominen, spent many hours doing the initial proofreading of the text as well as offering valuable comments. In addition to this difficult task, Lisa made the book a success before it even saw the light of day. After reading the draft, she told me that while the book did not make her decide to become a hunter or angler, it gave her a good understanding of the attachment that her husband, Josh, has for the outdoors. From my perspective, that alone, is a measure of success.

Doug Miller, Stu "Butch" Lakanen, and Rod Prusi all read the manuscript and offered valuable comments. Bill and Linda Walters were a great help in making the physical appearance of the book match what I had envisioned.

My wife, Sherilee, has been my inspiration, my friend, and my cheerleader, both in writing this book, and in life.

To each of these people, I offer my sincere and heartfelt thanks.

Introduction

I suppose my introduction to hunting, fishing, and nature was not something in my conscious memory. I undoubtedly heard my dad discussing these, his favorite hobbies, with his friends and my family before I knew what words meant. At some point I must have begun to understand what he was talking about and to absorb not only his words, but also the feelings he had for these pursuits. The lure of the outdoors has been with me from my very beginning.

I used to think that it was listening to these stories and being around my dad and others like him, that created my keen interest in the outdoors, but I have changed that view. Now, I really do believe that some of us are born with a desire for these things. If you are, it is in you to a certain degree from the very beginning, and just as there are some people born to sing or make music, there are some that are born to live the outdoor life. Your nurturing and environment certainly come into play, but if you have a strong, natural, "outdoorsy" gene in you, it is going to manifest itself at some point no matter where you were raised or who you were around. Maybe because of where you are and whom you associate with, it will be confined to watching birds and nature shows on the tube. However, more likely, you will find one or more outdoor pursuits that you will approach with a bit of passion. Just as a musician with natural talent and desire will become passionate and more skilled if he is encouraged and taught by those around him, so will the outdoorsy person react to a similar influence. That's me.

For almost my entire life, I have lived in areas where nature and good hunting and fishing were right outside my door. The family I was born into has a strong hunting and fishing tradition, as does the one I married into. The majority of the people I work with and who live near me are hunters, anglers, or nature lovers.

Much of my appreciation for nature came through hunting and fishing. These sports introduced me to the bigger picture. This is the case with many outdoor people. In one instance, this introduction came full circle. I was never really a duck hunter until I began watching ducks at a couple of ponds I had built on my property. I built the ponds to attract and help wildlife and spent a lot of time observing what was going on in and around them. Watching the ducks dropping out of the sky in the morning to spend a little time in the ponds captured my interest and sparked a desire to hunt them. I came to want to meet them on the predator vs. prey basis. When I did that, waterfowling moved quickly to the top position on my list of favorite outdoor pursuits. I watch the birds all year long and enjoy the watching immensely, but it does not come close to the enjoyment that I get from hunting them. It's that gene again. I love to watch a doe and fawn feeding in my hayfield or a family of ducks swimming single file through the cattails, and I will watch these sorts of things for hours. But I would rather get out of my deer stand and grab hold of the antlers of a buck I just killed or hear that smack of a fat greenhead hitting the water when I make that high overhead shot. It is primordial and you have it or you do not.

Chapter One
The Outdoorsman's Son

My friend and neighbor, the late Toivo Heikkila, once told me in his thick Finnish accent, "Yoo are da huntingest man I know." Toivo knew many hunters. I guess I know a couple of people who are "huntinger" than me, but not very many.

When and where I grew up, most dads were hunters, and most families rather expected that their young men would become hunters as well. I, for one, took to it well. My young pals and I talked and dreamed about the day when we could join our fathers in the field. For us kids, there was a mystique surrounding hunting. This was not so much the case with fishing, for even little kids can go along fishing with their dad. When my dad would come home from a hunt with some game in hand, I was fascinated with his stories of how he took it. I would watch him clean the birds or rabbits and often I took a foot or feather for myself as a souvenir, much to the horror of my mother. To this day when I clean a grouse, the smell of it triggers memories of standing and watching Pa as he cleaned his birds.

Once, he hung a red fox by its hind foot from our clothesline pole. I admired it hanging there, and I didn't know of anyone else's dad shooting a fox. He also shot a bear once, and I loved to look at the picture of him standing next to the bear hanging in my aunt and uncle's barn. There were also photos of some of my older sisters and cousins hamming it up by the defunct bruin. Not many people had killed a bear, but my dad had.

We had a hunting camp near Republic, Michigan, in Black River Location. In addition to being the deer hunting headquarters, we stayed there often during the summer. During our stays there, Dad would haul down from the rafters his old Winchester pump .22 and school me in the fine art of marksmanship. I remember how as a boy of about four, I would sit on his lap, him sitting on the ground, and let him steady that little rifle for me while I aimed. One time, we were using a coffee can for a target, and it had a small picture of a man imprinted on it as part of the label. He told me to aim at the man. When I dead centered it, he dragged that coffee can around for days showing it to all the uncles and aunts. Pretty heady stuff to have your hero bragging about you.

Dad took me along fishing from the time I was very small. I even was able to grouse (partridge) hunt with him when I was quite young, though I was a spotter and retriever and did not get to carry a gun. We spent hours and hours together in a boat, the car, or walking along logging roads. He was a quiet man, but we did have conversations. I learned from him to be content without conversation while in the field. Some people feel awkward sitting in a boat or a blind if there is no talking going on, but I can be happy as a clam just sitting there and watching what goes on around me. Not to say I don't like chatting, but I can do fine without it.

When we fished in the evenings or on the drive there or back, Dad liked to listen to the Detroit Tiger baseball games. The voice of the Tiger play-by-play man, Ernie Harwell, seems to play in the background of every evening fishing memory I have of those days. I listened to many Tiger games one summer, when we went on a camping trip to one of the state parks with Mom and my younger sisters. There was a good trout lake near the campground, and Dad and I fished it every night for the week or so that we were there.

The lake held both rainbow trout and splake, and on our first outing, we caught several that were from twelve to fifteen inches long. We caught them with spincasting gear, and there were only two lures in Dad's vast arsenal that got their attention. These were a small, red and white daredevil, and a gold-colored "hellgrammite." The latter had serrated edges and a slight bend in the middle of it. It was about one and one-half inches long. The hellgrammite seemed to be most preferred by these fish. We had only one of each lure. Each day, as we did other tourist things with Mom and the girls, Dad would pull over at every bait and tackle shop along the way to try to find more of the hellgrammite lures. The daredevils were easy to find, and we soon had plenty of them. Dad bought one of everything that even remotely resembled the hellgrammite, but we never did find any more of the exact one we were successfully using to catch the trout.

Each afternoon, we rowed our little flat-bottomed boat out onto the lake and fished into the night. As the sun went down, the nighthawks would come out to feed, darting and swooping all around us. The fish didn't hit much until darkness fell, and I grew a bit bored at times. I passed the time flinging my lure at any nighthawk that came close to us, trying to hit one of them. Dad was an intense angler and didn't really know what I was up to. Then on one of his casts, as the lure fell towards the water, one of the birds flew under the line as it was drifting down, catching it on its shoulder. The bird felt the line and panicked, turning to fly straight away from us as fast as it could. As the slack in the line was taken up, the bird pulled the lure right out of the water. I watched the lure shoot up and smack into the bird, and the bird went down with a splash. It fluttered a bit, got free of the line, and was airborne again. Dad laughed when I told him I had been trying all night to do what he had just done by accident.

The fish were great fighters, and this was about the most productive sustained stretch of trout fishing I had ever experienced. We ate a lot of fish on that camping trip!

The big show was deer season. Michigan opens its deer season on November 15 every year, and I remember well the preparation Dad went through for his annual week at the camp. The guns and the gear were kept in a little cubbyhole above the stairs, where I couldn't reach them, but I could view the guns. A week or two before the opener, Pa would haul down the box of red woolen clothes and go through them, I suppose to make sure all were there and that the moths hadn't gotten to them. Down would come his model 99 Savage, his cleaning kit, and an army surplus steel ammo box that held some compact binoculars, a metal hand warmer, cardboard boxes of shells for the Savage, his compass, and match safe. There were many other wonderful and mysterious little doo-dads that were saved just for the big November expedition.

I can remember the smell of Hoppes No. 9, and the hefty weight of the ammo box. I liked the shiny chrome finish of the gun-cleaning rod. These were like magic swords and potions to a young lad who had never made the November journey to deer camp. Dad could see my fascination with this ritual. As he wiped down the Savage with an oily rag, he grinned and told me stories of big bucks and old hunting partners and the days when he was a poacher. He told me that my Grandpa Prusi had killed a dozen or so deer in one day, and had once shot a buck that weighed, by everyone's estimate, 300 pounds, dressed weight. Everyone's esti-mate, that is, except my Grandpa's. He thought it weighed 325. He told how he himself had killed two big 10-point bucks in one day. The racks from those two bucks were stored in the rafters at the camp. I had admired them and run my hands over the gnarled antler bases and read the old, locking steel tags still affixed to the main beams. The fact that I can recall how enthralled I was with this activity speaks to just how impressed I was by it. Oh how I wanted to be a deer hunter!

Dad was a skilled deer hunter. I thought so then, and I have found out since that I was right. Many people have commented to me on how many nice bucks he took in the Black River area, which was his favorite hunting ground. He did not have photos of very many of them, and most of the racks had been discarded. There were three racks at the camp though. A nice wide 8-pointer over the door, and that pair of 10-pointers up in the rafters, perched on the rough-sawn boards, set down as shelves atop the logs that spanned the width of the camp.

When Dad was off at camp, we waited at home for news about

the hunt. Sometimes a telephone call would come, but Black River was a long distance call so even a trophy buck did not always rate a telephone call. More often, Uncle Bill, who lived right next door to us, brought news from the hunters. Other relatives would occasionally stop in with a report. One year, my little sisters and I were able to visit the camp during deer season. The girls and I mobbed the hunters at the camp, and one of them brought us out to the buck pole. With a flashlight, he showed us two nice bucks. This trip to the camp was like a brief glimpse of Shangri La.

I honed my limited skills with target practice and by roaming the woods around home. At age eleven or so, Dad allowed me to hunt grouse. I actually got a few by the time I was thirteen. Dad had created a monster of sorts. I was so keyed up to get "out the camp" for deer season, that I somehow persuaded him to let me come out the year before I was actually old enough to legally hunt deer. I was not allowed to actually hunt deer, but I carried my shotgun because rabbit season was still on, and I could make drives for the deer hunters. I managed to get one rabbit and be in on a successful drive, where my cousin, Rod, potted a little buck. I was able to stay for a three-day weekend, do chores, listen to stories, and take part in the planning for deer drives. Know what it's like to be out at deer camp for the first time and to hear one of the veteran hunters say, "We'll have Danny go in here..." as they planned an operation? This was a big deal for a kid like me.

A year later, I was actually a licensed deer hunter. Dad bought me a 30-30 Marlin in the spring, and I proudly kept it well oiled and ready for the season to come. I rode to camp with Rod in a heavy snow. Dad had gone there already to set things up. Rod thrilled me with stories of his hunting, he being a seasoned veteran of three seasons or so, who had already killed a buck. I still recall some of the songs that were on the radio. "Wichita Lineman" by Glen Campbell and Nancy Sinatra's "Sugartown." We got the green Chevy wagon stuck on the dirt road used as a shortcut to the camp. It took some sweat and shoveling, but at last we made it to camp.

Life at the camp during deer season was a much different world than the rest of the year. You were out with the men. There were no sisters to fight with, and I thought that if I bickered at all, I just might be sent home and not invited back. Nobody told me this, and maybe they would have cut me some slack, but I was out there with the men and sure didn't want to risk banishment by acting like a kid. Meals were basic, but large, and you could really put it away after a day in the outdoors. The women sent along plenty of bakery. There was always a good supply of chocolate, which never happened at home. Though this was meant for taking along as a snack when you were hunting, you always managed to down a bit of it at other times. The folks at the Negaunee Co-op store always threw in a box of chocolate covered cherries or something similar, at no charge, when deer hunters purchased their camp supplies there.

You had to be careful sneaking your cigarettes around camp, though, because you did not know when or where someone might go to take a leak and discover you sucking down your first Marlboro in several hours. If you were not careful on stand, the dads would see the unmistakable signs of your secret habit, they being expert woodsmen and readers of spoor. Speaking of smoking, the biggest hardship of camp life was running out of smokes and having to sneak one of Dad's menthols, which were awfully lousy smokes.

I only got in a couple of years of hunting with the big gang. That group consisted of Dad, Uncle Bill, Bill's sons, Rod and Chas, his son-in-law, Chuck, and me. Then we moved from our rural home into Negaunee. Bill and Jennie's family moved to Black River. Their men began hunting right from their house, and though we still did plenty of hunting as a group, the camp crew was smaller. For a year or two, it was just Dad and I. A few other friends joined us now and again.

In the spring of 1971, my folks were preparing to take a camping trip out west. Dad had always said he wanted to see the west before he died. Sadly, his wish would not come true, for he died of a sudden heart attack before the trip was realized. It happened only days before my high school graduation. I was prowling the woods and bluffs along the north side of Teal Lake, near home, with some

"The last Saturday in April every year—the trout fishing opener—found Dad headed to the Garlic after rainbow."

The outdoorsman and his son.
Walt and Dan Prusi.

of my pals that day. Far across the lake, the busy highway was visible. We heard sirens, and from a mile away, saw the ambulance drive into our neighborhood, then saw it racing back towards the hospital. When we were nearly back to town, my good friend, Gary Zanetti, was waiting for me with the news that Dad had been rushed to the hospital. Gary brought me straight to the hospital, but it was too late to say goodbye to my teacher and hero. There were still four of us kids at home at the time of Dad's death, and our lives changed forever.

While much of my recent hunting and fishing had been with companions other than Dad, we had always been afield together quite a lot. The thought of not being able to share those times with him, ever again, was no small burden to me. The very activities that brought me the greatest peace and contentment now brought feelings of sadness and longing.

The following deer season, I hunted at the camp with Bill Rowe and Denny Johnson. Bill Rowe had been Dad's best friend. That year, Denny had some battery-heated socks along and my cousin, Chas, commented, "Denny and his electric socks.....Sounds like a new singing group." The fun and excitement of the deer season had not gone away. There were tough moments, though. One evening, I lay on the bunk bed and stared at the empty rocker where Dad had always quietly rocked away the evening, listening to a high school ball game. I cried into my pillow that night.

The next fall, I hunted one more time at the camp, then during the season I moved to Minnesota, where I am today. I did not return to Black River for a hunt until November of 2001. My cousins, Chas and Rod, and their brother-in-law, Chuck Kovala, hunt out of the camp to this day, along with a pile of their boys. It is obvious that this next generation feels the same way about the camp that their fathers and I do. It is good to know that the family hunting tradition continues.

I lost Dad over thirty years ago. The sharp pain of grief has passed, but thoughts of my first hunting partner and teacher come to me often. Especially during those long, quiet times, in a deer stand or duck blind. I miss him still, but for the most part, these cherished memories bring a smile to my face and contentment to my heart.

Chapter Two
Friends and Teachers

The outdoorsman does so many little things with no more effort, or thinking, than he spends on breathing. Yet, someone has taught him each of these things. We come to realize this when we take someone under our own wing. When I took my boys afield, I quickly assumed the teacher role, and realized how much there was to tell. As I continue to try new things, I realize how many small details are involved with each new undertaking. There is no shortage of how-to books for the outdoorsman, and I have used plenty of them. However, there is no substitute for learning something by doing it, especially with someone who has done it long and well.

Naturally, as a kid, my dad gave me the most instruction in woodcraft and the fine points of hunting and fishing. Other men taught me as well. There were friends, uncles, and cousins. Some of the lessons I can recall clearly. One spring evening, I was catching a ride with my uncle Bill from Black River, where I had been fishing for a weekend, to my home in Negaunee. He knew I loved the woods and that I was interested in just about all things wild. As we left his home, he told me to watch the popple trees alongside the road as we drove along. He said there were sure to be partridge feeding in the uppermost branches at this time of day. Watch I did, and we began seeing the birds here and there as we drove. Uncle Bill explained that the birds liked to feed on the buds. I was rather astounded. Killing a grouse was a big deal for me back then, and to think there was anything as predictable as this with the birds was big news. Yes, it was spring, and it would not be the same in the fall, but still, here was a fact about grouse that was now filed away for future reference. Even then, I liked to watch game during the off season. As we drove along that winding road, I had my face against the car window for as long as there was light enough to reveal a bird on the skyline.

I have learned since that the grouse are after the catkins of the male aspen (popple) tree. In the spring of the year, the catkins begin to grow, and are a favorite food of the grouse. They will all but abandon all other food sources when these are available. Even today, when spring warmth opens the catkins, I watch the skyline at dusk. I still enjoy watching game.

Aspen, birch, and other tree buds provide food for grouse through nearly the entire year. None of these, however, commands the bird's total attention the way the aspen catkins do in the spring. In winter, the grouse are often in coveys, and one can see small flocks perched in a certain tree at dusk, taking their supper. Our Minnesota grouse season lasts until December 31, and for a couple of years, I took advantage of the evening budding to replenish my freezer. There were certain trees, especially birch, that seemed to be favorites of the birds, and I played sniper with my .22. That was a few years back, and now I feel like that isn't quite fair. However, I still watch.

I remember so many things that Dad told me. To wait, when a doe came along, because a buck might be just a few minutes to a half-hour behind her. How to look each fallen log over from end to end for a grouse sitting on it. How to back up to a tree when taking a dump in the woods during deer season. I started to laugh when he told me this, but he was dead serious. Flashes of white underwear might get some excitable hunter pointing his gun at you. He told me about situations where he had seen something he was sure was a deer and then realized it was a man. He had never taken a shot, or even raised the gun in those situations, but it had shaken him. I realized that if an experienced woodsman like him could make an identification mistake, I had better be double sure before I raised the gun and pulled the trigger. This caution likely cost me a deer one time, but I got praise from Dad for not shooting on that occasion.

My friend, Gary Zanetti, and his dad, Narcheeso, were the fellows who taught me a lot about rabbit hunting. Actually, snowshoe hare hunting. They took me along with them and their beagle, Sam. I knew a bit about the sport, for I had done a little of it. However, Cheeso and Gary hunted with their hound every weekend during the season, and they took the time to show me a few things. I knew that the hares ran in huge circles and that the hunter should find where it had once passed already, and to wait there for the dog to bring it around a second time. I learned about "strays," which are rabbits that are moving around because of the chase, though the dog is not on their trail. These can come from any direction and at any time.

I also learned a little bit about hunter's seniority rights from Cheeso. We were out on a hunt and had done well. We had a small pile of rabbits and had been hunting for many hours. We were a little distance from Cheeso's jeep, when with his little .410, he popped his fifth rabbit of the day. He had his daily limit, and he crowed a little because none of the rest of us had more than two or three. We had rabbits hung up here and there in trees so we didn't have to lug them around as we hunted. We asked our senior hunter, Cheeso, if he wanted to quit now that he had his limit. He said no; we would hunt for a while so that the rest of us might kill a few more. Then he sauntered off. Just a few minutes later we heard him holler to his son.

"Gary I'm back at the jeep. Catch the dog and bring the rabbits and let's get out of here." Therefore, as the boss warmed his toes in the jeep, that is what we did. I learned this lesson quite well. I feel no guilt when I subject my young and energetic charges to do a little more of the work than I do.

Certain moments in the outdoors never leave your memory. One winter my uncle, Chuck Prusi, invited me to join him and some friends on a winter rabbit hunt and ice-fishing trip to his camp. I jumped at the chance, and he picked me up on a Friday night after school. I had a little beagle pup at the time, named Sully, who I hoped to turn into a rabbit hound. Chuck and his dog, Lucky, were going to be our teachers for the weekend.

The days are short at that time of year. It was probably dark, or nearly so, when we left my house, and I know that after our thirty or forty-minute drive the sun was long gone below the horizon. The road to Chuck's camp was not plowed at this time of year, and it was covered with a couple of feet of snow. We had to hike in on snowshoes the last part of the trip. It was a hike I will not forget.

I had used snowshoes on occasion just for the fun of it, but this was the first time I really needed them to accomplish a goal. My dad had a pair that I had brought along, for Chuck had told me we would be hoofing it on the last stretch. It was one of those beautiful winter evenings in Michigan's Upper Peninsula.

It is difficult to describe the feel of the air on such a night. It must have something to do with the proximity of Lake Superior, and I imagine that it might be the same condition that leads to what they call "lake effect" snow. There is a feel, almost a smell, to the winter night. I have never noticed this where I now live, and I had forgotten that quality of the winter nights in the U.P. When my son was in college in Houghton, Michigan, I was reintroduced to this special feel of the night air. We made a trip to see him and stopped to do a little shopping when we got to Houghton. When I stepped out of the car, I was surrounded by the air of that winter night. A flood of memories came back. Memories of winter nights when I walked home from a friend's house or a school function, and how the night felt all around me. Feeling it again that night was like experiencing a sort of homecoming. My words cannot do justice to it.

That night we strapped on our snowshoes and hoisted our packs. I looked at the size of the pack that Uncle Chuck was carrying and was a little embarrassed at how little I could handle. I think I was about fourteen or so. I was clumsy on the snowshoes, but Uncle Chuck broke trail, and it was a lot easier for the second man in line. The skies were clear, the moon was full. There is a beauty to a moonlit winter night, when the evergreen boughs are laden with snow and the landscape smoothed by its white covering. The moon was bright enough to cast shadows, and the road was a white background with the eerie shadows of the naked trees crisscrossing it. There was no sound to break the stillness but the steady swish and crunch of our snowshoes as we steadily trekked towards the camp. Then, out of the stillness of that night air, came the sound of Chuck's hound taking the trail of a rabbit. For those who do not appreciate the magic of a hound's voice in full cry, this may have spoiled the quiet night, but for me the dog's voice completed a perfect setting.

Chuck paused to listen to his dog. I watched him there in the shadow-crossed moonlight. What a picture it was. A scene never observed, and thus not appreciated, by those whose adventures are only in a book or on the television. I love to read and to watch certain things on television. I love books and remember many of them well, but they can never etch something into your memory as clearly, as deeply, or as beautifully as will an experience like the one I had that night.

The dog was coming around. Chuck had been carrying his double barrel "broken down" and now snapped it together. I am not sure if he put in a shell or not. Shooting by moonlight was not exactly legal. He did not say anything but he stood and listened to the dog and watched for the rabbit. My puppy danced around on my snowshoes wondering what was going on. When the chase turned away from us, Chuck broke down the gun, and we continued on our way.

The camp was cold and it took a long time for it to warm up. The other members of the party arrived the next day. One fellow to do some fishing and the other, with his son, to hunt rabbits with us. We killed few rabbits, and I don't think we caught any fish. Nevertheless, it was a fun trip. What did I learn and take with me from this outing? Well, I was pretty sure Chuck was not above night-shooting rabbits, but that wasn't anything earthshaking. I guess what I took with me happened on that walk to the camp in the moonlight. A memory, a picture, that I will never forget, and a realization that in the outdoors, you will occasionally find beauty that no photograph, story, or song can ever describe.

Some lessons are not so much taught as they are learned, the hard way. We had moved from our rural home into Negaunee when I was about thirteen. When we lived out in the country, I had been given the freedom to roam the woods, even while armed and dangerous, with a .22 or my shotgun. When we moved into civilization, my gun rights were restricted, and I was none too pleased about it. This was especially difficult for me in the fall when the hunting season was on. I would get home from school on one of those beautiful fall days, and I could see the rocky, forested bluffs just a few blocks north of our house. They called to me! Dad was in his mid-fifties, and his job in the mine was still physically demanding. He didn't have the energy for hunting after work, so my hunts were confined to the weekends. When I was fifteen or so, I was in the yard one afternoon when he came home from work. It was one of those lovely days when the hunter will not be satisfied to do any activity other than hunt. Legally, a lad had to be seventeen to be able to hunt unsupervised, so I was still dependent on adults to get to the woods. I said hello to Dad and did a little whining about how nice it was and how I really wanted to go hunting. He looked at me and smiled, then pointed north, and said, "Well, there's the woods." I had been turned loose.

I am not sure I had a full appreciation for the trust Dad was showing in me. I was a young pup, and all I cared about was the fact that I was no longer leashed. Life was good. Each day after school I would hurry home, change, grab my gun, and be off. Mostly I went alone, but occasionally I was with other kids from the neighborhood. Sometimes we found a hound dog roaming the street and took him along with us to run rabbits. They always found their way home, and so did we. Mostly I hunted for partridge, but one year I began persecuting the ducks a little. My cousin, JR, lived at the farm where my dad grew up, just a mile or so from where I lived. We would hike from the farm, through the woods, to a lonely stretch of the Carp River, known as "the Troons." I loved going there. Dad had hunted and trapped there as a boy, so it was special to me. I don't know where the name came from, but isn't it a great name? "the Troons." A remote and lonely place for the average person, and a secret paradise for the hunter and trapper.

"Jay" and I took to hunting for ducks at the Troons one fall. There were many birds on the river. At the Troons, high, rocky bluffs overlooked the wide meadow where the Carp River wound its way on its journey to Lake Superior. On these bluffs, we found several man-made walls, constructed of flat stones piled about three feet high. The walls were short arcs and perhaps ten feet in length. They were obviously positioned to shield someone who would be able to watch the meadow below, and our imaginations created all kinds of stories about who may have built these walls and why. Indians perhaps, who were planning to ambush trappers on the river? Outlaws of some sort maybe? It added wonderful mystery to an already mysterious place. I asked Dad about the stone walls, and he said they had been there since he was a boy. The story he had heard about their origins was that deer hunters had built them to use as blinds when watching salt licks that had been placed there to lure the deer. This story was as appealing to me as an Indian ambush, and learning that the walls had been there since before Dad first walked the ground made them plenty old by my standards.

It was also said that this part of the Carp River had quicksand pockets that could swallow up a man. My dad told of a man who had stepped into one of these and saved himself by bracing his gun across some tree roots and using it to pull himself free. He then had to leap to solid ground, and the gun was left behind. It seems a bit implausible now, that he would not go back with a rope and retrieve his gun, but at the time, I believed every word of the story.

Another implausible story from the area was all too true. A game warden was murdered, just downstream from the Troons. It happened back in the 1930s, while the warden investigated illegal trapping activity. The killer was a neighbor of my dad, and well known to him. My dad was also an illegal trapper at the time. Dad's entire family had been questioned during the murder investigation. The grisliest part of this story was that the killer tried to dispose of the body by blowing it up with dynamite.

One snowy afternoon at the Troons, a neighbor lad and I saw a flock of Canada geese set down in the meadow some distance away. We attempted to stalk them, but were cut off by a shallow side channel of the river. I was only wearing knee high boots but my companion had hip boots on, and we were keen for a shot at the big birds. He suggested that he first carry the guns across and then carry me on his back across the water. With a possible opportunity at geese to think about, we gave no thought to the quicksand holes and we began to execute the plan. The guns made it across safely, and then I was picked up by my friend, who was smaller than I was. Part way across, his feet began to sink into the muck. In his efforts to free them he stumbled and went down, face first, into the cold water that was about two feet deep. Of course, I went down with him, but I managed to land on my feet and stay standing, only wetting myself part way up. I made for shore in the direction I was facing and in the process, walked up the back of my submerged partner. Man, that water was cold, but my pal came up sputtering and laughing.

We were soaked, and we had to abandon the stalk and head for home. As the saying goes, the longest of journeys begins with the first step. In this case the first steps of that journey home were the most difficult, for I had to wade back across that frigid slough! I didn't know anything about hypothermia back then, but I am lucky that I did not become a victim of it that day, for I had to walk about two miles to get home. It was one long and chilly walk. I could feel my gloves and pant legs stiffening as the moisture froze. I walked fast to stay warm and followed the blacktop roads wherever I could to save time, instead of sneaking back through the woods as I normally did. Maybe after doing that the first time, I started to get careless.

It was not legal for me to be hunting without an adult. It was hard to sneak the entire route in and out of town, for our subdivision was filled with homes, and it was a long three blocks to the woods. I didn't try to hide anything on that part of the route. I wonder now how many places there are where a teenager can walk down the street, with a shotgun, and not draw the attention of the law.

Once I hit the woods, I stayed off the roads. If I had to cross a road, I waited until there was no traffic in sight. I got careless the day that I took my soaking, but that was for good reason. Another time, I had no excuse for walking the road and it cost me. I was headed home from a hunt and took the easy route along the blacktop. When I heard cars coming, I would step into the brush and wait for them to pass. I was just stepping back out on the road from one of these evasive moves when I realized a second car was behind the one I had heard. Wouldn't you know, it was the game warden. I was busted. He was very polite and kind to me, but he wrote up a ticket, drove me home, and presented my dad with the summons. Dad, being my guardian, was responsible for the ticket. Dad was a little upset by this, but he was polite to the warden and not too hard on me, other than to shake his head over the fact that I had been walking along the road. A short time later, we, along with the warden, had to appear before a judge, in his chambers. Dad paid his fine, and he told the judge that he knew he had broken the law, but that he also thought it was a pretty silly law. The judge agreed, but nonetheless the law was the law, and it had been broken.

Lessons learned the hard way are sometimes the lessons that are learned best. I have been a relatively straight arrow on fish and game laws ever since.

Hunting and fishing were hot topics of discussion among my pals and me. It seemed like when I was getting to know a new kid, one of the first things I would ask was, "Like to hunt?" If he did, the conversation would take off. Where did he hunt? Had he ever gotten a deer? And of course, "What kind gun ya got?"

The first gun I ever shot was the Winchester .22 Dad kept at the camp. I still own the gun, and it is like an old friend. My first small game hunting was done with this little pump. I used it one season when I was about eleven years old. I wanted a shotgun, of course, but we were a big family and always pinching pennies. For my next season though, Dad found an inexpensive way to get me into a shotgun. He had an old 12-gauge single shot. It was light, and I learned later that it kicked like a mule. I was a skinny kid of twelve, and this would not have been a good starter weapon. I was not terribly eager to take on a 12-bore. Dad found that there was a little gizmo called a .410 sleeve that was designed to slip into a 12-gauge single shot, turning it into a .410-gauge shotgun. It only cost about twelve bucks. That was my first scattergun, and scattergun was an accurate term for the weapon, because the sleeve was only about fourteen inches long. Not much choke effect on the shot pattern with that setup. I hunted one season with the sleeve, but after we patterned it on a cardboard box, I think Dad realized I would do a lot better with a real shotgun.

My birthday is in July, and for a stretch of a couple of years, my folks had announced that we kids were going to get bigger, more expensive birthday gifts on a rotating basis. Because of the budget, not all of us would get the "big gift" the same year maybe, but we would all get a turn. It was the birthday after my "season of the sleeve" when my turn came up.

"Other men taught me as well. There were friends, uncles, and cousins."

The author's uncles, Chuck (on left) and
Bill Prusi.

We had a trip of some sort planned that summer that would find us away from home during my birthday. I begged my folks to get my present early. Dad seemed to like to toy with me sometimes, especially so if I was really begging. I kept getting a "We'll see." from him when I pestered. Finally, a few days before the trip, I was in the kitchen with Mom and Dad. I asked about my gift, and was surprised when Mom and Dad looked at each other, then Dad said to me, "Go and get it, it's under our bed." I recovered quickly from my surprise, ran to the bedroom, and fished out a gift-wrapped box from beneath the bed. The shape and weight of the box got me even more excited! I tore off the wrapping paper, and there was the box with "Wards/Western Field –

20-gauge Pump Action Shotgun" printed on the outside. What a day this was!

Dad had a twinkle in his eye when I ran out and thanked him and Mom for this wonderful gift. I had my first gun. It was mine and nobody else's, and it was a six-shot pump! I ran next door to show it off to my cousins. I read the owners manual. I checked out every line and button on this beautiful new shotgun. It was not expensive or fancy in any respect, but I doubt that I could have been more pleased. Dad got me two boxes of shells for the gun a short time later. I can still recall what the shells and shell boxes looked like. Plastic shotshell hulls were a brand new thing then. There was a box of number six shot. The shells were a deep reddish color with high brass and plastic hulls. These were for rabbits. The other box was number 7 1/2 shot for partridge, and they were yellow, paper hulled shells. At such a momentous time in a young hunter's life, no small detail goes unappreciated.

I killed my first grouse with my little twenty-gauge on the opening day of the first season I hunted with it. I killed four more later in the year. I was beginning to feel like a real hunter now. When I brought one of those birds home one day, Uncle Bill referred to me as a Nimrod when he was talking to Dad about my kill. Today, I am told, Nimrod is used as a derogatory description of someone. I don't quite understand that, for Nimrod comes from the Bible, and it was the name of a man who was a mighty hunter. So goes the world, I guess, but if you refer to me as Nimrod, I will not take offense. I know that the first time I heard it, another hunter was complimenting me, and it felt mighty nice.

Chapter Three
Brook Trout Hunter

From about the ages of 14 to 17, I spent more time in the woods with my pals than with my dad. This is normal for lads when they and their friends get their driver's license.

Pa really enjoyed fishing the spring run rainbows, usually on the Little Garlic River. The scene there was always kind of a zoo, with cars parked on both sides of the road starting a quarter-mile from the bridge and stretching an equal distance past it. This type of fishing required a level of skill that Dad had but I did not, and that, coupled with the crowd scene, soured me on the opening weekend trip to the Garlic. This is also the age when a guy is trying hard to be cool, which I failed to do on this particular trip.

I had been wading out to a little hummock of an island and fishing from it all morning. I would move around a little, but always head back to this little spot, for whatever reason. I was bored, and eventually I stashed my rod on the bank and just waited on my little island for Dad to be done and come back downstream. Finally he showed up, and when Dad was ready to leave, he was ready to leave. He was doing his seven-league boots walk as he passed by and announced—without breaking stride—that we were leaving. I hustled off the island into the stream and took a short cut to where my rod was. Only problem was, I had not taken this route before. Just one step off the hummock, in that direction, the water was about neck deep. I made a big splash and really impressed Dad and the fifteen or twenty anglers that were within sight. I have not been to the Garlic for the opener since.

The big splash took place about the time I got my driver's license, and our family had now achieved a level of economic independence that allowed us to own two cars for the first time in my young life. We had also moved to town, which after the first year was no fun for a woods bum like me. Consequently, the last Saturday in April every year—the trout fishing opener—found Dad headed to the Garlic after rainbow, and me headed for the Black, or another stream, after brookies. Usually some of my chums were along and we often stayed at the camp. Fishing for brooks was a little more in my league. Besides, if I fell into the river the audience would at least be smaller and familiar enough to me that I could go try to push them in if they laughed. My buddies and I fished, camped, bird hunted in the fall, and we still found time to go to Ishpeming or Republic to find girls to flirt with.

Girls distract a guy from his outdoor pursuits for a few years until you find one to settle down with. Then, if you pick well, you can really get down to being a serious outdoorsman.

Two of the guys I was with a lot were my cousins, Doug, and Kurt. ("That is Kurt with a K," as he always reminded us). Mostly we hunted and fished out of the camp, but occasionally we roughed it in a tent, and one long weekend was especially memorable. We pitched our tent on the Black River, down at "Big Hole" by the old Muustama farm. It is a beautiful piece of ground. Another of my cousins has told me he would give a certain treasured part of his anatomy for that piece of ground. The river flows through a long stretch of rapids, then empties into one of the wider pools on that part of the river. The entire river is thickly wooded, as most trout streams are, but at Big Hole, there is a large enough opening in the trees for a tent, campfire, and the various odds and ends that lay around a tent camp.

We spent a wonderful three days or so fishing, swapping yarns by the fire, and trying to poison each other with our cooking. One day, we heard a .22 going off and we followed the sound to see what was up. We met a man who was renting one of the old farms nearby. He was out doing some plinking with a .22 pistol, and he invited us to shoot a little with him and then stop in for a cup of coffee. We met his wife and a couple of their little kids. They fed us, asked us about our adventures, and treated us like grownups. I didn't realize it then, but the man had a twinkle in his eye that I now think was sparked by the replay we were giving him of the adventures of his own youth. They were nice folks, and I don't think I ever saw them again. One of the treats they gave us was deer tongue.

My pals and I were not into boozing, but we did smoke. Doug and I smoked those cowboy cigarettes, and Kurt smoked Winston. Whenever we were out in the woods and took a smoke break, Doug and I would sit down and slowly hum the Marlboro song as we lovingly touched a flame to the end of our cigarette. If we were by the campfire, we always took a long twig and dangled one end of it into the fire. When it started to burn, we used it to light our smoke, all the while humming that stupid song. Kurt would then grab a Winston in his teeth, crack open and fire up his Zippo lighter, and start singing the jaunty "Me and my Wi-in-ston, me and my Wi-in-ston" tune, taken from the commercials for his brand. He totally destroyed the mood.

Our first morning, we set out to explore and fish downriver. We had been drowning worms from the campsite almost since we got there and had caught just a couple of trout. Fishing was a big competition between the three of us, and cheating was part of the game. Good-natured cheating, of course. One of the big things you wanted to do was be the first guy at any good looking undercut, fallen log, or pool that offered promise as a hiding spot for a brookie. The trout that were in the mood to strike would usually do it soon after you got there, thus the urgency to be first. Now, if you came upon your partner at such a spot you quickly moved in and flailed the water with your own line, trying to beat him to the resident lunker. This was hole stealing, and it led to rapid progress downstream as each fisherman tried to be the first to new territory, and to leave the thieves behind. The first mishap of the day occurred when Kurt took up a position on a big rock that he waded onto from upstream. The eddy below looked pretty good. He got a nibble or two, which Doug and I noticed. Soon, all three of us were crowded onto the rock trying to fish. Kurt sneered with righteous indignation at having both of us steal his hole and stepped off the rock to head for fresh territory. He stepped off the downstream side though, and plunged in to a depth just a few inches deeper than his hip boots were tall. Doug and I found this very amusing.

We were a fair piece from camp, and Kurt wanted to get dry and warm. We had seen a shack on the far bank with a comfortable looking bench and a fire pit at the edge of the river. We decided to find a place to cross over, build a fire, and fish there like lazy men for a while. We moved upstream to a log we had seen spanning the river. Kurt pioneered the crossing and made it over without mishap. Doug was next, and about halfway across, the log started to roll. Doug never was, nor will ever be, graceful in the physical sense, so it was over quickly. He went in on the upstream side of the log and caught himself with his forearms to keep from going completely subsurface. Now the current was to his back and his lifeline, or "lifelog," was in front of him. His hip boots began acting like sea anchors and his butt like an underwater sail. The log naturally wanted to roll and let Doug roll underneath it like another piece of drifting debris. Doug got just a little panicky for a second, then got his act together and pulled himself along the log to the far shore. Kurt and I found this to be comedy of a high order, but I was forced to hold it in a little because I was not across yet.

I started across determined to remain dry while my partners were openly hoping for me to take a header off the log. I was trying to tune out their words of discouragement and looking down at where I was putting my feet. Suddenly, my pals were laughing hysterically, and I looked up to see that the log had pulled loose from shore at their end, probably from all the jostling it got during Doug's misadventure. Either that or they had kicked it free while I looked down at my feet. As I think of it now, that scenario seems increasingly plausible. My bridge to the far bank now ended in midstream as the current pulled the one end of the log away from shore. The log was now less stable than ever and started to roll again. I squatted down and dropped to a position straddling the log. My hip boots filled with the icy spring flow of the Black River, but from the thighs up, I was still dry. I looked at this as a successful tactical retreat with acceptable losses.

Having a small grasp of the principles of physics, I knew that I couldn't wiggle too far down the log without having it begin to sink. I instructed my pals to float me a pole, and although they really wanted me wetter then they were, there is a certain code of ethics among teenage fishing partners, and they were honor bound to assist. I used the pole to try pushing the log and myself back upstream a bit to the position it was in when I began this fateful crossing. The current was too strong. I pushed myself as far as I could towards my destination and then grabbed another pole held out to me by my partners. I "abandoned log" and Kurt and Doug reeled me in with the pole and slid me onto the bank like a half dead fish, soaking me in the process.

Wet, cold, and having the time of our lives, we jammed our wet clothes into our hip boots, and snapped the belt straps together on the boots. We slung them around our necks and headed upstream towards camp, where we had to swim back across. We got into dry clothes, got the fire going, ate, and sat back to hum the Marlboro tune. We had caught about three trout. It was a great outing.

For most young men, the kind of trip just described has a lot more appeal than fishing with their old man. However, I am happy to say that Dad and I did have one more fishing trip together in the spring of 1971, just a few weeks before he passed away.

We fished the Black, behind my cousin Nancy's place. It was just like when I was little, except I could keep up with him a little better now when we walked in. We hit the river where we always did and fished side by side at first, as we always did. Dad was to my right, and my line was in the water right in front of me and near the bank. Dad actually had cast in front of me to reach a deep pool on the far side of the channel from us. He immediately had a good hit but lost the fish. He baited up again and cast to the same spot, while I reeled in and waited for my chance. I made as if I did not notice what was happening and Pa was not gonna clue me in to the fact he had a good fish interested. The fish got his night crawler again, and this time when he reeled in to put another worm on, I dropped a lightning quick cast into the hole. This was hole stealing, pure and simple. The brookie hit immediately, and after a brief, violent struggle, we netted the biggest brookie I had ever caught.

I have told you Dad was quiet. When I got the fish in, I was excited.

"Boy he's a nice one!"

"Yup," said my dad.

"Man, I never caught such a nice one!"

"It's a nice fish."

"He's fourteen inches at least!"

"Thirteen."

"No, he's fourteen inches anyway."

Dad had not said anything about me casting into his area. He just pulled up a handful of green grass, and laid it in the bottom of his wicker creel. He laid the still flopping trout with its beautiful orange and white belly and colorful spots onto its bed of grass. Dad picked up his rod and cast another crawler into the dark waters of the Black, and without looking at me growled, "That fish is half mine."

I looked over at him, and he was just watching his line, chewing his gum, and grinning.

We caught a nice mess of fish that day and argued about whether my fish was thirteen or fourteen inches long. When we were done for the day, Dad dropped me off at my cousin Doug's place, where I was to spend the rest of the weekend hanging out with him and Kurt. I told Dad, when he left, to be sure to measure my trophy when he got home. The rest of the weekend was more fun and games with the cousins. It was late Sunday night when I got home, and the whole car trip home I was anxious to find out how big my fish had measured. When I got home, the first thing I said to Pa after hello was, "Did you measure my fish? How big was he?"

"No." he said. I asked if the fish was in the freezer, and he told me that he had eaten it. Then he added, "But it was thirteen inches." And he grinned.

I am mighty glad that I went fishing with my dad that day.

Chapter Four
Violatin'

Here in Minnesota, they call it poaching. Where I grew up, it was "violating." Everybody did it. Okay, not everybody, but almost everybody. If they were not doing it any longer, they had done plenty of it in the past.

By writing stories about poaching, I run the risk of giving someone ideas, but I sure don't want anyone getting the idea that I condone the practice. There sure are a lot of good stories about poaching, though, so I am presenting a few of them here. They are kind of entertaining, and like it or not, they are part of the history of hunting. Most of these stories take place years ago, when times were hard and deer were usually plentiful. We are also products of our times, and practices that are currently illegal, or that we currently view as unethical, were often accepted as normal in the not so distant past.

My granddad on my mom's side once got pinched for too many brook trout. He paid his fine but also lectured the warden for burdening him with a financial penalty for just trying to feed his family. They tell me that the warden had trouble looking Granddad in the eye from then on, and would cross the street to avoid him. I cannot be too upset with the warden. He was just doing his job, and especially in those times, it had to be tough to carry out his duties.

Feeding a family with poached venison was an accepted practice, at least locally, when my dad was a young man. My pa did his share of poaching, but gave it up in the last years of his life. When he was a young father, though, layoffs, strikes, and disability came along often enough to burden the budget. Like most of his contemporaries, he supplemented the food shelf with fall-harvested venison. He talked often and fondly about one fall when he was recovering from injuries suffered in a cave-in at the mine. He could easily have been killed, but a beam wedged against the side of the tunnel and kept the rock from crushing him. The beam itself crushed him enough to break his shoulder, and surgery was necessary. He had recovered from the operation enough to do most anything, but the doctor would not release him to go to work. It so happened that his cousin—and favorite hunting partner at the time—was in the same situation, with some burns on his arm. Pa would often relate the story to me and to others, grinning the whole time, as the fond memories brought a twinkle to his eye.

They fished on Lake Superior every week and on streams more often than that. They experimented with different loads for their guns, patterning buckshot and slugs in their shotguns to see which did a better job. They were planning to deer hunt out of season, but did not want to carry rifles along to make it obvious. If they were checked, they could say they were bird hunting. The shotgun would testify to that. That year, while "bird hunting," they took one deer each week. Either these two were overdoing it a little, or their families ate nothing but venison. They decided slugs were a much better choice than buckshot, and Pa killed one deer at 75 yards with a single twenty-gauge slug. He also clipped hair off one at 125 yards. Dad prided himself on his marksmanship.

Dad did some "shining" as well. He often mentioned how Uncle George Ruuska was the best shot he had ever seen—at night. Ordinary with a rifle in daylight, but when shooting in artificial light, Pa claimed Uncle George always hit his deer in one eye or the other.

Confession being the cleansing potion that it is, I will admit now that I have tried to kill deer out of season as well as at night, during the season. I just was not any good at it, and I gave it up while still a youngster, before I learned enough to be successful. If you hunt for the reasons I do, you will understand perfectly why I quit trying to cheat. There are several nice sets of deer antlers on my walls, as well as a number of spike and fork-buck headgear. I have saved every set of horns that I have taken. I love to look at them and remember the hunt as well as admire the beauty of the rack itself. If I had a rack from a deer I shot at night, or one that walked into the yard before season to get potted, not only would it bring back embarrassing memories, it would soil and contaminate the whole collection. I don't display the racks to brag, but I do like the fact that when people ask about one of them, I can tell them the truth about how I got it without getting red in the face.

Justice sometimes catches up with poachers in a form other than the law. A relative, who I will not name, has a poaching story that illustrates this. He was a young man then, still living on the farm with his folks. His dad was not above dining on early season venison, and the sons were avid outdoorsmen and eager to help with this particular harvest. One evening, my relative and his younger brother set out to shine themselves a deer. As they worked their way around the fields, the glimmer of eyes showed up in their light. The younger brother held the light and my relative took his shot. He made a clean, one-shot kill. Unfortunately, it was one of the family's cows.

Chapter Five
Hound Dog Man

When I was very young, we had a couple of hounds that Dad kept for rabbit hunting, and he had had several others before I was born. Hunting snowshoe hare with hounds was, and still is, a popular sport in Upper Michigan. When I moved to Minnesota, I was surprised at how few hound owners there were and how difficult it was to find hounds from hunting bloodlines. In the U.P., there were hounds everywhere, both for rabbits and for larger game. The beagle clubs there are still active today, and some fine hunting dogs are produced because of this interest in the sport. Dad spoke fondly of the good hounds he had owned. He also spoke about the fun of hunting rabbits with the dogs. Many of the hound men preferred bluetick or mixed breed hounds because of the snow depth that is normal in that area. Longer legged dogs can get the job done in conditions that would slow the little beagles down too much, or at least that was the reasoning.

Many of my friends were hound owners and rabbit hunters, and I was very keen on hounds. Dad subscribed to Outdoor Life magazine, which often featured stories about hunting with hounds; some of these were written about hunts that took place in Upper Michigan. In addition to the rabbit hunting stories, there were articles about hunting bobcat and bear with dogs. These were of great interest to me. Both of these sports were popular in our area. In a collection of old magazines, I still have some of my favorite articles on big game hunting with dogs.

In about 1975, I acquired my first real hunting hound. We had recently moved from an apartment in town to the farm where my wife had grown up. All country folk have dogs, and as a hunter, it seemed that mine should be a hunting dog. My mother, who was still in Upper Michigan, had told me that someone she knew had purebred beagle pups available for free. I had her reserve one, and some other family members picked him up when they were heading to Minnesota and brought him to me. I could tell immediately that he was no purebred, but he looked a bit houndish, so we kept him.

We named him Homer. As a lad, I had enjoyed Erwin Bauer's stories in Outdoor Life, and many of them were on cottontail hunting. They featured a beagle named Homer, so my hound was named after this famous dog. I spent a lot of time with Homer. I was in my early twenties, and what I lacked in outdoor skill I was able to, at least partially, make up with energy and endurance. I took Homer for walks and kicked brush piles in hopes that a bunny would run out and Homer would see it. We had a good rabbit population then, so we often managed to start one that way. Homer had the hunting instincts and would take the trail with me running along behind to watch and to help him when I could. The young dog relied on what tools he had—his nose and his legs. Like all puppies, and most young men, he did not use his brain at first. If the rabbit took a sharp turn, the dog would overrun the scent trail and begin searching. At times, I was able to see the trace of a well used rabbit trail and guessed that the rabbit may have followed it, so I would bring the pup over to this trail. If I was right, the dog let me know immediately, for a hound's reaction when it gets a nose full of scent is unmistakable. Their body language tells the story. The tail wagging picks up and you can almost see a slam of adrenaline shake their body. Eventually, it was best to let the dog work out these "checks" on its own, but for starters I did what I could to help.

I read up on beagles and talked to anyone I could find that had hound experience. I took my dog in the woods every chance I got. I picked up freshly killed rabbits on the road, brought them home to drag around the yard, and let the dog follow the scent. The work paid off, for Homer turned into a pretty good dog. I can recall when he drove his first rabbit to the gun. My wife's young cousin was hunting with me, and Homer brought a rabbit around on a short circle. Mark made the kill, and Homer was blooded.

I kept notes, just as I do now, regarding my hunting. I kept a stat sheet on Homer. I recorded each hunting day and how many rabbits were taken. I noted whether the dog drove them or if they were strays, which were rabbits that moved due to the chase that was going on, even though the dog was not on their scent. If we killed an incidental rabbit—one with no contribution by the dog—the dog got no credit. Many of my pals would join us for hunts and all seemed to enjoy watching Homer do his stuff. I think it was during his second hunting season that Homer drove his 100th rabbit to the gun. We marked the occasion with a small celebration and presented a makeshift certificate to my brother-in-law, Phil, who made the kill.

I added another dog to the household when I bought Sam, a registered beagle from excellent hunting bloodlines. Sam was named after another dog from my early years, the dog owned by my friend, Gary Zanetti. Sam was a lot slower on the trail than Homer, but he would often pick up the scent when Homer overran it. He was from field trial stock, and these dogs are bred to work out the trail without overrunning the scent. I preferred the hard-charging style of Homer, for the chase moved quickly and the rabbits often came by at a dead run, making for sporty shooting. Sam had real difficulty with trailing on snow. I knew he was good on bare ground, but I did not realize just how good, until I lost Homer.

It was 1977. I hunted with the dogs in the morning and took a couple of bunnies. Shortly after we got back to the house, Homer seemed disoriented and unresponsive. I made a bed for him in the porch and he lay down there all afternoon and evening. I checked him frequently, and he seemed very ill. I considered whether I should take him to the veterinarian in the morning. As silly as this may sound now, I had been raised not to "waste money" on dogs, especially with something so frivolous as a vet. By morning, Homer was gone. Whether a trip to the vet would have saved him I will never know, but to lose a dog that I had developed such a bond with was a very difficult blow. I have had many dogs since Homer, and when they have problems, they are transported quickly to a vet.

Not long after losing Homer, Phil and I made a hunt with Sam. It was a beautiful fall day, and it was my first hunt with Sam going solo. When an athlete has a day where he performs far better than anyone expects, they say he played "out of his mind." That day I thought Sam was out of his mind. We hit the woods and he took a trail almost immediately. The scent was holding well, and the dog was giving voice steadily, never losing the scent. Sam was not a babbler, which is a dog that bays or barks even when not on scent. If Sam was singing, there was rabbit scent in his nostrils. When he was on a trail, he did not push them very hard, but he pushed them steady. His entire hunting career had been spent with Homer out front, until there was a check. Then Sam would often come in and save the day. Well, on this day it was his show, and what a show it was.

I have photos from that hunt. In the pictures are seven bunnies and a grouse. (Sam also retrieved wounded grouse.) Sam was on scent almost constantly that morning, and all seven of those rabbits were driven to the gun. No strays and no incidentals. I don't think he took a trail that did not end at a dead rabbit. We had to have shot well, for it was not an all-day hunt. However, Sam was the star, for he pushed each of those rabbits to the gun and stayed on the trail as long as it took for one of us to shoot it. It was his chance to show his ability, and he did me proud.

Sam had other good days, but never did well once the snow came. He was only with me for a few seasons before dying from gastric torsion, the turning of the stomach. Homer and Sam were good hounds. It would not have been inappropriate for me to include them in the Friends and Teachers chapter, for the three of us learned about hounding rabbits together.

I had a steady parade of hounds for several years. Susie was a tiny little hound with lots of drive, and she had a habit of stopping and standing up on her hind legs to look around and sniff the air. She was paired with another dog, Fritz, who was the best trail hound I ever owned. They had several litters of pups together. Fritz was sure on the trail, and he was the only beagle I have had that understood and enjoyed the concept of being part of a team that included a human. All of my hounds ran rabbits and seemed to know that the longer they stayed on the trail, the better chance they had of eventually tasting some fur. However, they hunted for the joy of the chase and would trail rabbits for hours whether they had a gunner along or not. Fritz liked being with me. He would run a trail for a half-hour or so, and if he had not seen me in that time, he would come to check on me. If I was still hunting, back to the trail he went and picked it up again. If I had started for home, he would trail me until he caught up or got back to the house and then stop for the day. I could call him off a rabbit, which was not anything I taught him, but as I said, he liked being with me and understood the team concept.

Most of the hound men I knew did not train their dogs to "come" on command. It is an easy thing to teach a young dog, so it is well worth teaching. Do as I say, not as I do! Often my hunting was done near my home, and we walked to and from the hunting area. If the dogs were still in the mood to hunt, I let them hunt until they had had enough. They would return to the house when they were ready. If I wanted to save the dogs' energy for a hunt the next day, or if we hunted somewhere farther from home, I had to catch the dogs when I was ready to leave. This was sometimes the hardest part of a long, hard day, and my pals and I made some spectacular tackles in the snow to get the hounds leashed. Sometimes we just could not catch them. If I was a long way from home, I just stayed for as long as it took to get the dogs. If I was only a few miles from home, I used a tried and true hound man's trick. I put down one of my coats in a sheltered spot near our parked vehicle, drove home, and returned after dark. Invariably the dogs were waiting for me, curled up on the coat.

Keeping the dogs deer-proof can be a bit of a challenge, though by no means insurmountable. I never owned a hound that did not end up deer-proof, though a few of them strayed off the straight and narrow occasionally in their youth. Some dogs are never interested in deer; others have a weakness that you have to work on. Homer had an unhealthy affection for deer scent. His deer habit was strong, and I had to deal with it.

We were then living at my wife's old home place, which was still an active dairy farm with fields surrounding the house. In the evening, the deer could be seen feeding in these fields. I took my "problem child" to the field one evening with a twenty-foot rope tied to his collar. We got downwind of the deer and walked quietly through the woods to within fifty yards or so of the animals. I walked slowly into the field, and stopped to let the dog snuffle around. He smelled and then saw the deer, just as they saw us and fled. He took off like a shot after them. I yelled "No!" once or twice, but the dog never broke stride—until he got to the end of that rope. His head and neck stopped, but his body continued on beneath them, and he was on his back with a thump. He sort of staggered to his feet, rather disoriented, and I was all over him before he could regain his composure. He got a few swats and was led promptly and roughly back to the house. The next evening I tried the same thing. This time, he saw the deer but did not bolt until the deer saw us, snorted, and fled. Then the temptation was too great, and he streaked after them, only to hit the same barrier as he had the night before, get another spanking from the boss, and another grounding at the house. On evening number three, we did the same routine. The dog saw the deer, and the deer ran off. The dog looked at the fleeing deer, then up at me, and then he sat down. I never knew him to chase another deer.

I am told that in the south, there are hound men who run their dogs on fox. The entire sport is the chase. No guns are carried, and there is no intent to harm the fox, unless he is slow enough or dumb enough to be caught by the dogs. These fellows will loose their dogs and sit by a fire, listening to the chase, picking out the distinctive sound of each hound's voice, and judging by ear how each dog is doing. Hound music is what we call it. I love listening to the sounds of a hound on the trail, as do all hound men, whether it is a pack or just one dog. I occasionally did this listening routine with my beagles in the off season. I would walk out behind the house, often with a buddy, in the evening. We would light a fire and let the dogs go. We would sit by the fire, drinking coffee, discussing the mysteries of life, and listening to the music of a lively chase under clear and starlit skies.

All hunting dogs see rough duty, hounds perhaps rougher than any. Rabbit hounds are always forcing themselves into thickets to start a rabbit, and once the chase begins, they are moving fast, over unfamiliar ground, through all kinds of cover. I saw plenty of injuries and got to be fairly good at first aid. Once, as I waited for the dogs to bring a rabbit around, I heard a vicious fight break out. The two dogs bellered and growled for ten or fifteen-seconds, then were silent. I called to them, and in a few minutes, they came to me. One of them had his ear badly shredded and had several cuts on his face. I will never know what sort of critter opened that can of whup-ass on my dog, or why. Perhaps some predator, an owl or bobcat, had spotted the rabbit that the dogs were trailing and killed it. When the dogs came up, a fight may have ensued.

I have had three dogs disappear while they were hunting. On one occasion, I was hunting with a single dog and all morning I had been cutting fresh coyote tracks. These tracks were sometimes found over my own tracks that had been made just fifteen minutes earlier. It was late February, when coyotes are mating. About the time I decided it would be wise to quit the area because of the coyotes being so bold, I lost touch with the dog. I never heard or saw him again. There are documented cases of beagles being killed by coyotes, and our area has its share of "greater coyotes," the big eastern timber wolves. Another of my dogs survived two separate maulings and both times the fang marks I found on him were so far apart that it had to be a bear or wolf, unless it was perhaps another domestic dog.

One of my dogs ran a stick into the inside of her mouth while in hot pursuit, and because of where the wound was, I could not find it. I had heard her yelp, got to her, and checked her over closely, but could find nothing wrong. After a day or so, the side of her face was terribly swollen. A trip to the vet revealed the wound, and the dog recovered quickly. Another time, one of the hounds came out of the woods to me, cowering. This was very unlike her, so I walked to meet her. When I knelt down, I saw that one eye was badly swollen. I could see something protruding from the corner of the eye. She seemed to know I was trying to help, and let me take her head in my hands and tilt her nose up towards me, so that I could see what the problem was. It was a twig, just over a quarter-inch in diameter. About a half-inch of it was protruding. I sat down beside the dog, held her neck under my left arm, and cradled her snout in my left hand. She never flinched or made a sound as I took the stick with my right hand and slowly drew it out.

The stick was almost two inches long. Later, at the vet clinic, we saw that the stick had been driven in, alongside the eye, rather than into it. The dog healed and never had any vision problems that I could detect. Hounds are rugged dogs.

When I first became a hound dog man, I spent many weekends in the off season just taking them out for a run. When the small game season opened in September, I always kicked it off with a rabbit hunt. The dogs got plenty of work throughout the fall, with a break during the rifle deer season. During the long holiday weekends, we again hunted a lot over the dogs. After New Years, there were two full months with nothing to hunt but rabbits, and we persecuted the big hares with determination. The rabbits were abundant during these years. There were many days when a dozen or two found their way to a place of

"Sam was the star, for he pushed each of those rabbits to the gun and stayed on the trail as long as it took. He did me proud."

Cedar Valley Sam, on his greatest day.

honor, on our belts.

Some days, it seemed that the rabbit scent hung thick along their trail, and the dogs could run almost flat out without overrunning. Other days, I could put the dogs on a track that I had seen the rabbit make just moments before, and the dogs could not hold it. It is one of those mysteries of nature and science as to why one day can be so different from the next. It seemed to me that moisture in the air helped the conditions for the dogs, and the absolute ideal conditions seemed to occur when we had those big, fluffy snowflakes, falling thick and coming straight down. It was as if the dogs could run in full cry with heads up and never lose the scent. The chases were long and fast, and when it was headed your way, the heart would race as you tried to spot the moving white rabbit in a landscape that appeared to be all white and all moving. In such conditions, the rabbit could be right on top of you before you knew it. Usually, it spotted you about the same time you spotted it. It would streak off, presenting a challenge to your marksmanship. The nicest thing about this situation was that even if you missed, you would just get to listen to more hound music as the dogs continued the chase. A good hot chase that lasts a long while is more fun than killing a rabbit anyway. Moreover, I will take hound music over country-western music, any time.

Chapter Six
A Measure of Success

Like many young hunters, my early years were filled with clumsy, stumbling efforts. These efforts seldom yielded much in the way of game. Good opportunities did not often present themselves to me, and when they did, I often dropped the ball. Such is the case for many of us when we start out.

What success I had came mostly with trout, grouse, and rabbits. Even at that, it was seldom that I returned from a hunt with more than one dead critter. Those occasions when I killed two of something were my first "great hunts." They were rare. I should add that during my first years of hunting, the grouse were at a low point in their cycle, and deer were mighty scarce around our hunting camp. I suppose, that in finding game so scarce while listening to my dad's tales of killing five bucks in one season, that it made me think I had to work a whole lot harder on my hunting skills.

During those first years of deer hunting, I went through two consecutive seasons in which I never spotted a deer. Another year, I got two quick shots at a very nice buck as he streaked across a gasline right-of-way, over a hundred yards away. Another time, I missed nine shots at a huge doe that casually walked back and forth on the gasline about 350 yards away. I got a lot of teasing about that one, but at least I got in some trigger time.

In spite of this lack of success, the hunting season was a most wonderful time. To be hanging out with the men, and deer hunting, was about the best thing life had to offer. The years when Uncle Bill's family stayed with us at the camp were the very best times that I had there. Rod and I took a lot of teasing from the "old men" who were veteran deer hunters. We made drives, got lost, and helped to drag out the rare kill. I missed a fox one time. After the painful years of waiting for my chance to hunt at the camp, even the paucity of deer could not spoil such a wonderful experience.

My dad, along with nearly all the veteran deer hunters, believed that the best recipe for success in deer hunting was to spend long hours "on watch." As a youngster, I got cold easily, and suffered a bit from boredom as well. However, I wanted a buck and knew that stand-time was necessary to make that happen. When there were opportunities for more active types of hunting, though, I loved it. Deer drives were fun. I was able to move around if I was one of the "dogs." If I was lucky enough to be one of the "standers," the idea that there were other hunters out there attempting to chase a deer to me made the stand time much easier to take. I never had an opportunity to shoot while I was on stand during a drive, but once, while acting as a dog, we had a very exciting time.

I was on the drive with Chuck Kovala, who was married to Rod's older sister, Kathleen. Chuck was one of the veterans and had me under his wing for this drive. Dad and some others were on stand at the gasline. Rod, and another cousin, Lenny, were also dogs that day.

Not long after the drive began, shots began to ring out. At each shot, Chuck and I would stop and wait, looking around in hopes that a deer might come into view. This never happened, but the thought that it might kept me very intent on what was going on. I was also very anxious for the drive to end, so that I could find out who had shot at what, and perhaps get to see a deer carcass.

When we emerged at the gasline, Dad said that he had missed a shot at an antlerless deer when it had stuck its head out of the brush, far down the gasline. The rest of the shots had come from Rod. He and Lenny had jumped a couple of deer and had been able to come up on them several times. Rod killed a yearling buck, and he and I carried it out of the woods.

Another exciting hunt occurred a few years later when Dad winged a buck that had come across the gasline near his blind. Dad had been looking in one direction, and when he turned back, this buck was almost into the woods, having made it nearly across the opening while dad looked the other way. There were pieces of bone and blood on the trail where Dad has shot the deer. There was little snow. Warm weather and slight drizzle had melted the inch or two of snow that had blanketed our hunting ground earlier that weekend. After Dad directed other members of the group to stand sites where he thought they might get another shot at the deer, he and I took the trail of the wounded buck. I suggested to Dad we take along a shotgun, with buckshot loads, for we might get an opportunity at the buck in thick brush or as he bounded away from us. Dad elected not to do so.

We trailed with not a little difficulty. After a short while, a second deer apparently joined up with the wounded animal. I was enjoying this immensely. I knew that there was a buck at the far end of these tracks, and with it wounded, I might get a look at him. Perhaps I would finish him off. That would help my standing in the group!

After an hour or so on the trail, we were trying to unravel it in a spot where the snow was completely gone. Two deer bolted from thick brush just a short distance away. I couldn't see them, but Dad saw that one of them was running with difficulty, and fired a quick shot at it. He missed, and we took up the trail again. After several hours, we were unable to follow the tracks any longer. I was discouraged, but not nearly so much as my dad was. I now know exactly what he was feeling, for I have been in the same situation. On our walk back to the camp, he expressed his disappointment in his shooting. In his prime, he said, the buck would have been dead on the gasline from a single shot. He also told me that he should have listened to me when I suggested the shotgun. This made me feel as though perhaps, I was learning a bit about being a deer hunter.

The following year, Dad killed a nice 8-point buck from the same blind where he wounded the buck I just told you about. When we looked the deer over, there was a funny abscess of some sort on its brisket. We thought that perhaps it was the same buck that Dad had clipped a year earlier.

With deer as scarce as they were in the late 60's, when we stumbled onto one, we often pursued it with some determination. One might say, desperation. Such was the case one morning when one of our group stumbled onto the track of a lone deer between the gasline and the camp. The track was that of a decent sized deer, and given that it was travelling alone, we thought the odds were good that it was a buck. Hunters were dispatched to various stand locations, and I volunteered to track the deer. As mentioned, I enjoyed being able to be more active.

I had heard many a lecture on the importance of the hunter remaining in his stand. If I left my stand before I had spent what the others thought an appropriate length of time, I would always hear about it. I had also been raked over the coals for moving too fast on a drive. Some of this was sinking in. As I took the deer's trail that morning I was determined to do this assignment as instructed. That instruction was simple. Stay on the tracks.

There was no challenge to following the tracks, for there was fresh snow and no other tracks around to confuse with those of my quarry. I moved along the trail slowly, hoping I might catch a glimpse of the deer myself, and perhaps get a shot. Tracking is fun work that I still enjoy doing today. This was probably my first real attempt at chasing down an unwounded animal. If we got the critter, I knew that one of those on stand would most likely make the kill. I did not mind this at all, for I would get some credit if I pushed the deer to the lucky hunter.

The Black River country is rugged. While the hills are not terribly high or steep, the valleys below are often choked with alder brush and sometimes wet enough to challenge the passage of the hunter. I persevered. One foot got wet when I went over the top of my boot. I battled through alder thickets, trying to remain quiet. At last, I saw that I was nearing one of the men on stand. I knew that several others were not far away, and it seemed as though I might give one of them a look at the deer, which had never bedded. As I neared an old gravel road where one of our group was to be on stand, I heard the rumble of tires on the gravel. I looked up, and through the trees and brush, I saw Dad's car pass by with all the hunters inside. They had given up on waiting for me and were heading back to camp.

Moments after the car passed from my sight, the crashing of brush gave me a start. I caught a flash of brown hide and white tail as my deer bolted across the road, only seconds after the car had passed. I had done my job, but the veterans had given up on me too early. Perhaps they thought I was lost in those swamps, but when I finally got back to camp after hoofing it a couple of miles, they weren't forming any search party. I told the sad tale, and for once, it was acknowledged that I was the one member of the team who had done his job properly. I was not angry over the missed opportunity once I got my due on the performance. Here was another case where I was starting to feel a little more like a genuine deer hunter.

It wasn't long before I finally got my first deer, and I wish I could tell you that there was a lot of hunting skill involved in that momentous occasion. There wasn't.

It was several days into the season. Perhaps the second weekend. There had been little deer movement in the area surrounding the camp. As he often did, Dad decided that we needed to look for greener pastures, so we left the camp before daylight to go "out east." This was the area east of the town of Republic. Dad had often hunted this area with some success. We brought along a lunch, and spent most of the day there. In the afternoon, we headed back for the camp. When we were just a few miles from camp, I spotted a doe and yearling alongside the road on my side of the car. We were on Grape Hill, so named because many years before, a truckload of grapes had overturned on the hill. The deer were on the hillside, thirty-five yards or so from the car.

"Deer!" I blurted out.

Dad stopped the car as I began uncasing my 30-30 and fumbling for a shell. I rolled down the window, got into a kneeling position on the seat, slipped in a shell, and aimed at the larger deer. She was quartering sharply away from me, standing on the steep hillside, and looking back over her shoulder at us. The yearling stood broadside, just a little behind the doe. There was not a good angle for a chest shot, but that didn't worry me. I let the front bead settle into the rear sight, and placed it between the deer's eyes. I pulled the trigger. The doe's head snapped back, and she went down in a heap with hardly a quiver.

"Did you shoot it in the head?" Dad asked.

"Yeah!" I said, as I smiled back.

"The hunting season was a most wonderful time. To be hanging out with the men, and deer hunting, was about the best thing life had to offer."

Walt's Camp, near Republic, Michigan.

Dad shook his head and smiled. We got out and gutted my first deer.

Now at the time, I was proud of my first deer. Obviously, the way I shot it was illegal. One does not shoot from an automobile. Just as obviously, there was not a lot of skill involved in the hunt. We were driving down a paved road when we lucked onto two deer. Now you know why I am a little embarrassed about my first deer.

Though I have not killed a ton of deer, I have done reasonably well collecting venison over the years. Every deer I have taken, other than this first one, was taken in the field rather than from a road. While a certain amount of luck is involved in every successful hunt, all of my other deer were taken legitimately. None were taken while "road hunting." None were taken after they just wandered into my yard. I am a little proud of that, just as I am a little ashamed of how I got my first one. In fact, there have been times, during open season, when I have spotted a buck from my car, or outside my living room window. I don't even search for a weapon. I do not feel quite right about shooting a deer that way. Maybe I am doing penance for my fist deer. Perhaps one day, a huge buck will wander into the flowerbeds at the house and tempt me. I cannot promise you that I will not try to shoot him, but I hope I do not.

During the same season when I road whacked my first deer, I had another successful hunting encounter. While it had elements of luck similar to the deer story, there was nothing illegal about it, and it was a totally sporting hunt.

I had set up a watching spot on a small, rock bluff, just off the gasline right-of-way. It wasn't much, just a cushion of balsam boughs on the rocks with an old stump to lean on for a backrest. Below the bluff, I had seen a lot of deer sign. There was no wide vista from this perch. I could see only about fifty yards or so, but the amount of sign in the area convinced me it was a good spot to spend some time.

I had sat here in the early morning hours one day, then returned to the camp for some lunch. In the early afternoon, I returned with the intention of staying for the remaining daylight hours. As I approached my cushion and began to sit down, I saw a movement below. A coyote had bounced up from a bed beneath a blowdown, perhaps thirty-five yards below my position. Obviously, my approach had disturbed him, but not to the degree that he raced off. He got up and was walking briskly across my front. I got my little 30-30 shouldered and tracked the little wolf in my sights as he moved through the brush. When he got to an opening, he stopped and looked up towards me. If he saw me, it was the last thing he ever saw. I shot him between the eyes, just as I had the deer.

The coyote fetched me a $15.00 bounty check. I had brought home venison and cash, all in the same season. I had a long way to go in becoming a hunter, but at last, I had experienced a measure of success.

Chapter Seven
The Bow Hunter

The doe was cautious. After each mouthful or two of clover that she pulled, she would raise her head and look cautiously about, then take another couple of steps forward. One more look around and she would take another few bites and repeat the performance. Her fawn, plus another doe and fawn, followed behind her. The three followers were less cautious, but they stayed well behind the larger doe. She was obviously in charge of the group and relied upon to spot the danger. Twenty yards away, just off the edge of the field and under a large balsam, I shivered in the cold October drizzle. I was seven days into my career as a bow hunter, and it looked like I was going to get a decent crack at a deer. Earlier in the week, I had missed several shots, all within a hundred yards or so of where I was now waiting in ambush. I was seeing my 76th deer of the week. This foursome had entered the long narrow opening only minutes after I set up in the balsam trees. The dark shadows hid me well, and a decent opening in the brush would let me get an arrow through to any deer that walked along in the narrow field. I had no elevated stand, I just leaned against a tree.

There had been oats sowed in this small field. They had been harvested only a couple of weeks before, and the underseeding of clover was now lush and green as it flourished in the new-found sunshine and the sudden lack of competition from the oats. It was drawing deer like a magnet.

Opening day in this field had been a real circus, with my brothers-in-law and me playing the roles of the clowns. Deer were everywhere, and both Greg and I had missed close shots in the morning, then I missed again in the evening. All day, we heard the sounds of blowing deer, the drumming of hooves, and the occasional twang of a bowstring followed by the clinking sounds of arrows hitting brush. We had a wonderful time. Now I was watching the field alone, and this small group of deer had been headed towards my shooting lane for the best part of an hour. Finally, the doe looked like she was taking that last step into the opening, and I began to draw my recurve. She stopped and looked at me! The bow was half drawn, and she was not yet clear of the intervening branches. It looked like I was had. It seemed like a longer time, but I am sure it was only a few seconds until the deer put her head down for another nibble or two. I let off and had a chance to take a breath. Then she entered the shooting lane, and I took aim. She was twelve yards away. I actually aimed beneath her brisket, because the deer earlier in the week had been jumping the bowstring at my shots, dropping as they coiled for their first jump. Now, at the twang of the string, she tore off in the direction she was facing. She circled around and into the woods, just beyond a point of trees that reached, like a peninsula, into the field. She did not look hurt or overly alarmed. I walked out to where she had been standing to look for sign.

The other three deer were still standing there, looking around somewhat stupidly. I didn't try to shoot. I just shooed them away. I looked over the ground where the doe had been standing when I shot and saw no sign of a hit. I headed into the woods on the opposite side of the field to a sandy strip of ground. I thought I could cut her jump marks in the sand and begin to track her. I nearly tipped over, for I spotted the doe lying dead in the middle of the trail. I ran over, pretty well delirious with joy. I laid the bow down and knelt next to her. I stroked the fur. I looked at her black nose with the white trim around it. I turned her over and looked for the arrow. No arrow here, just a clean X on each side of her chest where it had passed completely through, killing her in just a few seconds. I had killed a deer—only my second—and I had done it with a little 45-pound recurve bow and a cedar hunting arrow. I could not believe it. When I dashed into the barn to tell my father-in-law, busy with his milking, he didn't believe it either. I finally convinced him and ran into the house to get a knife so I could clean my trophy. It was 1977, and I was 24 years old.

That is what launched a second chapter in my hunting career. Up until then, I had been a successful grouse and rabbit hunter (not exactly big league stuff there), but a real bust in the deer-hunting department. When I moved to Minnesota, it was new country, new people, and a new style of hunting. Deer hunting was not quite as fun as it used to be. Perhaps it was because my surroundings were all brand new, from the landscape to the people I hunted with. The landscape was fine deer hunting ground, and the people were great. I guess I just like familiarity. I started to go more my own way, and I thought that hunting with a bow would be fun. It would also give me a chance to deer hunt a lot of prime territory all alone, before the big gangs of rifle hunters took to the woods. Getting the deer that first year was just what I needed to restore my confidence and to remind me what, for me, is the most rewarding part of the sport. I am not talking about getting a deer; I am talking about challenging deer, or other game, and competing with them. The actual ritual of the hunt is its greatest appeal. Learning the animal's secrets. Infiltrating their hidden world without them knowing you are there. There is nothing like it in the world.

After this first successful season, several of us banded together to become a dedicated group of bow hunters. The members changed some over the years, but the real die-hards, for a long time, were my two brothers-in-law, Tim Tuominen and Phil Hyry, and a good friend, Jim Shubitzke. We took vacation time in the fall, got together a lot, and even pitched tents for a week every year to bow hunt. It was a great party. Brother-in-law, Roger Johnson, and my cousin, Rod Prusi, were regular members of the group. Many others joined us for a season here or there.

We killed a fair number of deer over the years and learned a lot about hunting them. If we get together and swap old yarns, as hunters tend to do, there are many yarns to be swapped. The same is true of any group that has shared many years afield. Sometimes one particular season provides a disproportionate number of good stories. Such was 1987.

It was late October, a snowy Friday. The annual campout was about to begin. If memory serves, I was the first one to arrive at "Kurki's," a piece of land my father-in-law owned at the time, and where we had begun holding our camping and bow hunting week. I brought out a motor home that we were able to borrow, and set it up. The first couple days of our campout were always the time we would bring along our kids. I cannot say enough about the veteran hunters, who had no kids to bring along, and how they put up with the racket and inconvenience of having all these little buggers tearing around camp. They all should be in the Uncle Hall of Fame.

After setting up camp, I went out on stand. I wasn't far from camp, and I quit early and returned to camp because of the ever-increasing din as others arrived. Jim was there with his boys and mine. Cousin Rod arrived with one or two of his sons. Jim was in the process of setting up his tent. (Jim turned his nose up at the motor home or popup camper we always had.) He liked the tent with its cooler air and being able to hear things hooting and howling during the night.

As things settled a bit, we started to prepare supper. Suddenly, Phil came bouncing down the two-rut road in his car. He leaped out, all in lather, and waved his arms, because he had stuck a "nice 8-pointer" over at Marty's farm. He had seen this buck earlier in the season and had been playing the chess game trying to get a shot. Tonight, he had connected. The snow had been falling all evening, so we thought the tracking would be easy. Phil assured us that it was a good kill shot. We held a brief council of war, and Jim generously offered to stay and get supper ready for the kids while Phil, Rod, and I went to recover Phil's trophy.

The tracking was indeed easy. The hardest part was keeping Phil in sight as he barreled along the blood trail in quest of his first good buck with the bow. Soon we had the deer, or I should say we had a deer. Although it was obviously a deer recently slain by an arrow, it was not the big 8-pointer we were expecting. However, it was a good 6-pointer, big enough to get me tired dragging it to the car. We razzed Phil a bit about how the rack shrunk to a 6-point after death, or maybe this was someone else's deer. All the other bucks he had killed seemed to get bigger over time, yet this one had shrunk. He just smiled. There is nobody more difficult to irritate than the man who has just killed his buck. This was a darn good start to the campout, in that we would be able to have a kill talk around the fire the first night, and venison tenderloin for supper. This we did, once we were back at camp with the buck hung up. Phil's success added to our enthusiasm, as often will happen when one of the group scores.

After that first weekend, Rod and all the kids pulled out. Tim and Roger were now in camp with us. It was the first morning after the kids had left. Phil (already successful) was sleeping in. Jim was in a favorite spot in a portable, and Tim was out at his favorite permanent stand. Roger had set up a portable northwest of camp in an area where a buck was doing considerable scraping. I was not feeling confident that day. As always, I was hunting many different stands, and as luck would have it, none were proving too productive. I got up that morning not knowing where I was going to hunt, which is very unusual for me. It tends to sap my confidence, and I should know better. Hunting is the kind of activity where lady luck smiles upon the dumb at very unpredictable times. At the last minute, I chose to go to one of Tim's permanent stands that was only a couple of hundred yards from camp. Once before, when I had been in this state of low confidence, I had gone to this stand, and ended up having a close encounter with a doe and two bucks, one of which was a monster. The three had thrashed me that day. Perhaps it was the memory of that beating that kept my confidence low as I got into the stand just before shooting light.

The stand was a permanent wooden structure, built in a small group of balsam and aspen trees. The woods immediately surrounding it were open and mostly aspen, with some balsam mixed in. Thirty yards to the north, the ground dropped sharply into a wide creek bottom, filled with brush and swamp hay. Fifty yards east was a natural opening in the woods with nice grassy cover. That creek bottom was a good bedding area. I stood in the stand, my bow hanging from a handy stub of a limb. It was a nice, sunny morning, and it was pleasant to quietly observe the surroundings from my perch, although seeing a deer was not something I really expected. I was just low on confidence for whatever reason. It had only been full light for a half-hour or so when all that changed.

As I turned to look north, a decent buck had just come up the bank from the creek bottom. He was standing and working some overhanging balsam limbs with his rack, doing the routine they do when they are on a scrape. He did not scrape, but he worked those limbs with his rack and rubbed them on his face as he deposited his scent onto the branches from the pre-orbital glands. It was a pretty picture. It has always amazed me how a person's body is slammed with adrenaline at a time like this. It is transformed instantly from a lazy observer to a keyed up, fully alert predator. I have had times when it felt like it would knock me out of the stand.

I was able to pick up the bow and get it into a ready position. After only a minute or so, the buck began walking towards me. As he approached, I could see that he was reaching a fork in the trail. If he went to his right, he would be in cover, and there would be a good chance that he could walk by without giving me an open shot. If he went to his left, he would pass nearly broadside at about ten yards. His choice was great for me, very bad indeed for him. I was able to draw and take my shot without complication.

The arrow struck with a thwack, like a baseball bat hitting a wet blanket hanging on a clothesline. I hit him too high and too far back, and he rocketed to the east through the little clearing. I had made a poor shot and was convinced I had gut shot him. I was disgusted with myself. I waited just a few minutes, got down, and walked over to the last place I had seen him. There was good blood sign, so I marked it and headed towards camp. I thought I would alert the crew, and we would wait for a couple of hours because of the gut hit. Then, we would take the trail.

I reached the logging road that ran by camp, at the top of a hill, fifty yards from the campfire. I could see that Tim and Phil were there, and they spotted me.

"He's laying right there!" they said, pointing behind me.

"What's right there?"

"Your buck!"

"Not my buck, my buck is gut shot!"

"No, your buck is laying dead right there in the balsam trees!"

They got up and walked over to me. They led me twenty yards down the road, then off to the side just a few steps. There indeed was my buck, deader than a mackerel, with my arrow sticking out of his side. He was a nice wide 6-pointer, with real beams rather than the glorified fork-horn type 6-pointers. He ended up weighing about 150 pounds. My arrow had hit the liver, and he had only lived five or ten minutes after the shot. Phil and Tim were laughing and congratulating me, and they told me the story of how my buck had stumbled almost into camp and then died ten feet from the road.

Tim had been on stand before light, and at first light a nice buck, bigger than the one I had just killed, walked into his stand sniffing the ground. He shot and hit it high in the chest, the buck tearing off and pulling all the string out of his tracking device. He had hung his bow in the tree and headed directly back to camp. There, he roused the dreaming Phil. He told him to get up and make him some breakfast so they could go out and recover his big buck. Phil, roused from his dream world, got up, and the two of them got the fire going and began preparing breakfast. As they did, Tim related his morning's adventure. Sometime during the course of this debriefing, Phil looked up and spotted a buck standing on the road.

"My word, there's a big buck right there!" he whispered to Tim. Tim had left his bow in his stand, and Phil's was put away somewhere, so there was a mad scramble to find a weapon. By the time Phil armed himself, the deer had meandered off the road, so the two of them stalked the area where it had gone into the woods. Phil says he could not believe his good fortune when he spotted the deer lying down! He had already killed a good buck, and now the smiling Gods of the Hunt had delivered another to him right in camp! He was about to draw, when Tim brought him down to earth.

"That deer has Dan's arrow in it." he said, and as the deer breathed its last, Phil saw the arrow protruding from its side. They looked over the kill, and if I remember right, Tim had to dissuade Phil from putting another arrow into it for insurance. They returned to their meal preparations, and a little while later I wandered in with my chops dragging on the ground over my gut shot buck. As you can imagine, we had a good laugh then, except maybe for Tim who had his own wounded buck out there, still to be recovered. Phil commented that if he and Tim had been smarter, they would have tossed my buck into the back of the pickup, told me it was theirs, and kept me going for a while. I replied that the only reason I continued to keep company with him and Tim was that they were not very smart.

Well, the story does not end here of course, because we still had to go after Tim's buck. This we did, and that bugger led us on one of the wildest tracking adventures we have ever had. There was no blood at the beginning; in fact, we did not find blood until we got to the far end of the string from the tracker. Then there was very little, but enough to keep us going. We placed people on stands a few times in the hope of chasing the wounded buck by them, but that never happened. We tracked and tracked, heading further and further to the northeast. Finally, we knew we had to quit. It was nearly dark, and we saw that the buck was making scrapes, in spite of being wounded and pursued. We packed it in. Tim went back the next day and tracked some more, and even the third day he cut its blood trail again for a while. Unfortunately, we never got that guy. Fortunately, he seemed not to be hurting too badly, and we hoped that he would recover.

Later in the season, just before the firearms deer season was to begin, I hunted a stand behind my father-in-law's place for what was to be my last bow hunt of the year. Roger was hunting the same general area, as were a couple of the others. Minnesota allows party hunting for deer, meaning that if a group is afield together, one person can take more than one deer, as long as the party has valid tags for each deer taken. I was hoping to get some venison for the others in the group who had none yet.

My stand was a permanent wooden structure about nine feet off the ground and ten yards from an old logging road that the deer often traveled. Almost beneath the stand was a well-used deer trail that crossed this road. There was no seat in the stand, and little room. The hunter had to remain standing throughout his watch there. As darkness began to settle around me, I spotted a nice doe coming down the logging road towards me. The stand was in thick balsam cover, so it was much darker than it would have been at the same time in surroundings that are more open. I got set and watched the doe approach, debating whether I should take a shot, or wait to see if there might be a buck on her trail. The rut was underway, so the odds of that being the case were definitely worth considering. She walked to the intersection, turned, and passed on the trail right below the stand. I decided not to try a shot, for there was still some time left before sunset. She slowly passed out of my sight.

Perhaps fifteen minutes later, I heard the thump and rattle of a deer approaching from the direction where the doe had disappeared. Suddenly, she trotted back down the trail and stopped below my stand, looking back over her shoulder. I only had a few minutes left in my season and this big doe was now in a perfect shooting position, six yards from my tree. I took the shot and saw the arrow drive deep into her chest. She was off like a rocket.

I listened intently, trying to track the deer's location and hopefully hear it fall. The silence of the evening closed in around me, and I could hear nothing of my wounded doe. I waited quietly for several minutes, still straining my senses to try to hear the deer. Slowly, I became conscious of a very subtle sound from the opposite direction. It is funny how when you look or listen for a particular thing, something that does not match what you are trying to locate will sometimes escape your conscious attention. That is exactly what happened, and I suddenly realized that this tiny, strange sound had been there for a few seconds. It was coming towards me, on the same trail that the doe had come down. Suddenly my reasoning got in gear; it having been somewhat dimmed by the adrenaline rush of shooting the doe.

The doe had been spooked back towards me and had been looking back over her shoulder when I shot. It was rutting season, and the sound was moving along the doe's trail, and when I finally listened to the noise I was hearing, I recognized it as the strange, creaking grunt of a rutting buck. Now the second slam of adrenaline hit me. I began reaching for another arrow from the bow quiver, at the same time trying to turn to a position where I could take a shot. I was too slow, for he was already right below me! He saw my movement, spun around, and trotted back out of sight, though he did not dash off in great alarm. I got the arrow onto the string and got turned, hoping that perhaps he wasn't too spooked. It was only a few seconds later when he came right back down the trail and into the shooting opening! I began my draw, and as I did, he jumped a little, seeing or hearing the movement. To my surprise, he just kept moving with his nose down near the ground, sniffing the trail of that doe. He was only three yards from the stand, and it was a very steep angle down. I let go my arrow and it hit with a loud whack, the buck (a 4-point) springing away at the impact, straightaway into the spruce bog just off the deer trail. To my further surprise, the buck stopped and blew at me several times! This was very puzzling. Perhaps there was a third deer back there.

Well, now I was into it. Two wounded deer to follow. As I looked down from the stand, I was amazed to see my second arrow sticking straight out of the ground. I immediately thought I had hit a rib or shoulder on the buck and the arrow had been deflected downwards, probably doing little damage. When I got down, I saw that the arrow had blood and hair along its length and there was a little clump of deer hair on the ground where the arrow had hit. I walked out to get my pals.

Tim and Roger got excited when they heard my story, and we headed back to the stand and began tracking immediately. I knew the doe was well hit, so we started on her track. The first sixty yards or so was tough, with little blood sign. The arrow had hit high and perhaps not penetrated completely through. Once we found blood, we found progressively more and more as we tracked. Once or twice, I was sure I heard a deer bound away just ahead of us, but it was hard for me to believe that this doe was alive. After just a few minutes of tracking, we began to see the unmistakable evidence of a killing lung shot. Frothy blood, in ever-increasing quantity, sprayed on the ground with each exhalation. We found her easily, and she had died within seconds of receiving the arrow. We dressed her out and went on to blood trail number two.

We found little blood. All signs pointed to a bone shot that kept the arrow from penetrating. The buck had stopped and blown at me, and I was sure that he had continued on the trail of the doe even after I shot him. I am sure it was he that we heard when we were trailing the doe. We quit his trail pretty quickly with confidence that he was in no great danger from this wound. Our judgement proved to be correct, for my wife's cousin, Doug Miller, killed this buck just four or five days later during the firearms season. I heard he had killed a fork buck that had a fresh wound on its left side, so I stopped by to look at it. On the deer's left shoulder, high on the shoulder blade, was a jagged but partially healed hole. About eight inches below that, there was a second hole. I had brought along the arrow, and when I put the broad head up to the entrance hole, the V shaped cut matched the broadhead blade profile perfectly. The arrow had deflected off the shoulder and exited eight inches below where it entered.

As mentioned in the beginning of this chapter, 1987 was quite a year for exciting stories. Phil took a buck that is his best archery trophy, although it seemed to shrink between the time he shot it and the time we found it. I took two deer, including my second best archery buck. The tracking of Tim's buck was the longest tracking adventure we have ever been on. However, these were not the best stories from that year. The best story, is the strange case of Moonlight Jim.

As you will remember, our first night in camp in 1987 was eventful, in that Phil killed a nice buck. It was a snowy night, and Jim had remained in camp to fix supper for the kids while Rod, Phil, and I had gone out to have the fun of tracking. This all took place after dark, so by the time we returned to camp, hung the deer, and had our supper, the three of us were pretty bushed. Jim still wanted to go out to put up a portable stand, to sit in, in the morning. None of us old guys had the energy to join him, but my son, Danny, and Jim's son, Josh, went along with him to erect a portable by flashlight. The rest of us turned in for the night. Jim and the boys returned about 11:00 P.M. and went to bed.

It was a cool night, and the snow continued to fall on our little campsite. As the snow stopped, the fire flickered out, and darkness and quiet settled around the camper, motor home, and tent. I would imagine that Phil was sleeping with a wide grin on his face. Most of us didn't sleep real well the first night in camp. New surroundings, excitement, and a cooler sleeping environment led to tossing and turning. After a couple of days of hard hunting the sleep would come easily, but the first night or two were usually restless ones for us. This night was typical. The quiet was interrupted several times by people getting up to stretch, snack, or pee. For me, it was one of those nights when it seemed I did not sleep at all, except for thirty seconds just before the alarm went off. When it did, the bow hunters were all up and at 'em, getting their gear together and preparing the light breakfast that was customary on serious hunting days: instant oatmeal with coffee and bakery, or some other quickly prepared meal. After a few hours out on stand, most of the crew would come in for a proper breakfast, like eggs and bacon.

For some reason, Jim was not out of the tent. We called to him several times and got no answer. Finally, Danny responded to my last wakeup call by saying that Jim had left a long time ago. That seemed a

"Sometimes one particular season provides a disproportionate number of good stories. Such was 1987."

The author (left) and Phil Hyry, with their 1987 bow kills.

little funny to the rest of us, because it was still black dark and plenty early. Jim's stand was one of the closer ones to camp, so he had no reason to leave earlier than the rest of us. We were also a little chagrined that he got up, ate, and left without waking any of us. Oh well, we thought, let's go hunting. So we did.

I spent an uneventful morning watch perched in the strangely shaped top of a huge balsam tree. The top had broken off years before. The "star" of horizontal limbs, below the broken terminal branch, had all taken off vertically and formed a multiple top. They were far enough apart to give a bow hunter plenty of room to sit in the midst of them. By clearing a few limbs away, I had shooting possibilities on several trails that wound through the surrounding, heavy, balsam cover. The ground was snow-covered from the previous day. With no deer movement around me, I headed back to camp after a couple of hours.

When I arrived at camp, Phil was puttering around the fire as he always does, but smiling a little bit more than normal. I thought he was still basking in the afterglow of hunting success, but when I commented on his expression, he laughed and told me the real story of what had him amused. It turns out that Jim, after returning from stand building and getting to bed late, had not slept too well either. At one point he checked his watch and found that it had stopped. This worried him a little, as he did not want to oversleep the first morning of our hunt. Apparently, he did not want to rely on the others who had the alarm clock. Fretting over this, he got up and went to check the digital clock radio in his new Chevy truck. When he pushed one of the buttons, it said 6:10 A.M. Holy Smokes! He thought. I did oversleep!

He went over to the motor home to wake the rest of us and saw all the tracks we had made during the course of our midnight snacking and the answering of nature's calls. Now he got a little perturbed (I surmise) because he thought we had all left for our stands and had not bothered to wake him. He quickly gathered his gear and headed off to his stand. It was not a long walk, so he was on stand in just a few minutes, where he settled in to wait for shooting light.

Wait he did. As he told us later, he watched the eastern horizon to look for lightening skies, and when that did not happen in a while, he snoozed a bit. It was clear now, and cold. Jim would wake up, wait a little bit, and snooze some more, but snoozing was not easy in the chilly black of night. We figured later that it was about 3:30 A.M. when he got into his stand. The readout he saw on his clock radio in the truck was AM radio station 610. Well, Jim had no way of knowing what time it really was, so he just stuck it out.

A half-hour or so before dawn, Rod walked under his stand on his way to his own spot. Rod was unaware of Jim, and Jim never bothered to say hello. It is fortunate he stayed quiet, because when you are walking in a dark forest, the last thing you need is someone calling out your name from above.

To Jim's credit, he toughed it out and stayed on his stand for a couple of hours after daylight finally arrived. We were as impressed with Jim staying on stand for that length of time as we were amused at his snafu. It was fodder for a lot of giggles and razzing for the rest of the week's campout. Jim probably got the biggest kick out of it, because several times, as I watched him around camp, he just started to chuckle and shake his head. He described many times for us how long that morning had been, waiting for sunrise and watching that eastern sky just staying dark.

Yes, 1987 was a year of unforgettable stories. That of Moonlight Jim will be the last one we forget.

Chapter Eight
Bears

I have had an interesting association with bears over the years. I was terrified of them when I was small. I am just a little bit afraid of them now. As a kid, I seldom saw a bear, but I heard plenty about them. Dad had shot one, and everybody had bear stories to tell. In Upper Michigan, there are plenty of bears, and the rural nature of the place brings people in contact with the bears frequently. Most bear stories concerned running into one while berry picking or trout fishing, and getting the crap scared out of you, or of garbage raiders that met their end on someone's porch in the middle of the night. When I was a kid, our neighbors killed one that way. Everyone in the neighborhood walked or drove over to get a look at it hanging in a tree, outside the home where it had chosen to go after one garbage can too many.

Once, as a youngster, while waiting for the school bus with my cousin, Audrey, we had a bear encounter. My kid sister, Sue, was walking up the road towards us from the house, when we heard crashing brush in the woods alongside the road halfway between Sue and where we stood. We looked into the woods, and a brown colored bear jumped up onto a large, flat rock. We were terrified and yelled to Susie to run back home, which she was happy to do. The bus was pulling up so Audrey and I were saved from what we saw as certain death. Everybody laughed at my story because I said we had seen a brown bear. Only black bear lived in Upper Michigan. I did not know about the brown or cinnamon phase bears that appear occasionally, and I am sure now that that is what we saw.

Another time, while staying at the camp, the folks had gone out berry picking. The blueberries were abundant that year, and we always picked a lot for Mom's baking. When they returned, Dad mentioned that there was a lot of bear sign in the berry patch. The bear, or bears, had been feeding on the berries and turning over logs and rocks to gobble up ants and grubs. My fascination turned to horror when Dad said that he and I were going back there to get more berries, after he finished his lunch! Now I was only seven or eight years old, but even then, the male machismo was forming inside of me. I sure couldn't tell my hero that he would have to brave the bears by himself and pick berries while I stayed at the camp with Mom and the girls. I swallowed hard and went along.

Normally when I was picking blueberries, I spent more time wandering around looking for bugs or snakes than berries. I suppose Dad wondered why I was so willing to stick by him and keep picking that day. I was always looking over my shoulder, figuring a bear was stalking me. We picked in a little glade surrounded by young saplings. I have mentioned before that Dad was a quiet fellow, and we did not chat at all as we picked. Dad was happily filling his coffee can with the blue treasures, and I was all keyed up, scared to be there. Unbeknownst to us, a doe had come along to feed in the clearing. I don't know how long she was near us, but suddenly she snorted about twenty yards in front of us. I was up and streaking for the car quicker than I can tell you about it. Pa got a good belly laugh out of that one.

I have had at least three occasions where a camping trip was made livelier by visits from a bear. One year at Camp Cozy, the spot where we had our annual bow hunting camping trip, a bear rummaged around the camp all night. Tim and I were having a ball watching it and yelling at it until we got tired and just went to sleep. Phil was there and somewhat bored with it all, until in the morning when we found that the bruin had sat on and destroyed his popcorn popper. Phil was then ready to track the bear down and kill it.

A few years later, in the Boundary Waters Canoe Area Wilderness, our party was totally cleaned out of food by a bold raider that lounged around camp all day within a few feet of us. This was a real bummer because we had a long way to paddle and portage to get out of there, and nothing in the way of fuel in our bellies. We got to the cars and still had to drive an hour to a restaurant. There, we ordered one of everything and pounced on it like a pack of wolves, almost before the server set it down.

Just a week or two later, I was on another camping trip with my sons. Another black bandit pilfered a loaf of bread from us before I could drive him off. Besides robbing some food, he stepped on, and broke, a fishing rod that I had owned since I was twelve. At least that one did not keep coming back as the other camp raiders had done.

Naturally, being an adventurous and outdoorsy type who lived in bear country, I eventually took to hunting the critters. The first time was a public service. Marty, my father-in-law, had one of his steers mauled by a bear, to the point where he had to ship it to slaughter. We were living at the farm then, so I decided to buy a bear license, try to bait in this outlaw, and end his criminal career. This was in about '77, the same year that I got into bow hunting, and before I became as meticulous in my hunting preparation as I am today. I baited in a poor spot and with the wrong stuff. I was not consistent enough with my baiting. No luck. I tried again the next year, and I did better, but not by much.

One time, a bear cleaned up the bait pile.

After a few years' hiatus, I tried again. By this time, I was big into bow hunting, and had read a lot about baiting bears. I decided to try with my bow and spent more time in selecting a site, finding proper bait, and providing the bait regularly. I did some drags, pulling a rag soaked with grease drippings and bacon fat from several directions in to the bait. I hung anise and liquid smoke soaked rags from limbs above the bait. It wasn't long before I had one or more bear visiting the site daily.

The stand site was just off my back field, only a half-mile from the house. I had a portable stand in a big balsam tree just ten yards from the bait pile. Before the season had opened, one bear had climbed up into the stand to check it out. We have found that bears do this a lot, for whatever reason, and we even had a deer stand we called the "Bear Shit Stand" after the calling card left us by a visiting bruin. I had practiced shooting from the steep angle you get at ten yards from an elevated stand, and by opening day, I was feeling confident. Maybe too confident.

The second or third night on stand (I seldom sit for bear in the morning), a smallish bruin came in. It was fascinating to watch him glide in on noiseless feet, swinging his head from side to side to test the air. He nibbled up green plants growing on the ground as he moved in. We tend to picture a bear as smashing along through the brush. In fact, when you run into one, that is usually exactly what we see and hear as the bear flees. Here though, was an undisturbed bear, moving in to feed. He was as quiet and stealthy as any buck deer. There he was, eight yards away and right in my shooting lane. I missed him. Sweaty fingers. Too excited. Bad angle. Shot over the top of him. I was just unglued and let go with my eyes wide open, and I don't think I saw the bow sight at all. If the bear came in with stealthy grace, he left with graceful power, gone in a flash with hardly any noise.

It was one of those times I was left shaken, wondering how the heck I could have loused up such a great chance. I calmed myself down and stayed in the stand, probably more to compose myself than anything else. Before I had even fully calmed down, a second bear ambled in! Might this be a chance to redeem myself? He moved in to almost the same spot where the first bear had been, and I shot under him. Twice. The bear left, and at that point, so did I.

I will tell you plainly that this whole episode left me wondering if I should ever hunt with a bow again! That one evening still ranks as my worst hunting performance of all time. It really made me question my ability. I am happy to say, I recovered. Our annual Labor Day trip interrupted my hunting for a couple of days and allowed me to put the big blunder into perspective. When we returned home, I resumed my hunting. The bears had not been frightened away from the bait. After all, what was there to be afraid of?

The next evening out, I settled in the stand and started my vigil, not really hoping a bear would come in. I won't say I hoped for no action, I was just kind of in neutral. Sitting on stand in the early

September bear season has a completely different flavor to it than deer hunting. Flies and mosquitoes buzz around you, and often sweat is trickling down your back. The sweet smell of anise, smoky bacon fat, and bug dope always seem to be present. More of the summer birds and bugs are around, adding different sounds to the atmosphere. It has a summery feel to it rather than that of autumn.

Before long, one of the bears showed up. He came in much as he had the previous visit. He was quiet, slow, and nibbling plants as he came. This time however, instead of going right to the bait, he walked over to the stand tree, sat down in front of me, and looked up! He sat there a while and then turned to go to the bait. I remember very clearly, two odd things about this encounter. The first was when he sat in front of me and looked up, his beady little eyes spooked me. For a little while, they looked sinister, but then they just looked a little stupid. I know that bears are generally neither of those two things, but that's the impression I had at that moment. The second odd thing was when he turned and walked straight away from me to the bait. His rear paws turned up as he lifted them, like he was going on his tiptoes, and the whole sole of the foot faced me. Not significant, but just a couple of little details that stand out in my mind. He moved to the bait, lay down on his belly, broadside to me, and began nibbling on a cookie that he held between his paws. I drew and let the arrow go, and this time I hit. The shot was a little far back and low. The arrow hit and deflected downward and rearward, exiting on the bottom of the bear's body and driving deep into the soft ground. At the impact, he leaped to his feet with a fierce snarl and rocketed into the brush, pulling string out of my tracker so fast that it made a hum until it broke after just a few seconds. Then it was quiet except for the buzz of the insects and the songs of the birds.

I got down from the stand and headed to the house where I called my neighbor, Jim Liubakka. Jim came over to help me track, and it was dark by the time we started. We followed the tracker string and some minimal blood sign for only thirty yards or so when we found the broken end of the string. Very little blood was to be found at that point, so we decided to let him lay for the night and pick up the trail in the morning. That is just what we did, and when we got to the bait we saw that another bear had been on it and completely cleaned it up. So now, we had at least two bears to consider, one of which might be dead or wounded. We started trailing and were joined by another friend, Paul Ostervich, a short while later.

The trail led into a cedar and alder swamp, and the blood petered out quickly. We fanned out to try to pick up the trail and for several minutes, there was nothing to be found. Then Jim and Paul called me over to them. They were standing just a few yards from an uprooted cedar. The roots had pulled up, and sod and dirt had been drawn up with them. This formed something that looked like an igloo; a cozy compartment covered with sod and roots and with a two-foot diameter entrance hole on one side. Another hole, half as big, could be seen on the top. The bear, they said, was inside this little compartment. They had both seen the bear clearly when they had looked into the top hole. They were not sure if it was alive or dead, so I approached with caution and with my 30-06 raised and ready.

I looked into the top hole and saw nothing. I looked into the side hole and saw nothing, but the view of the interior was not very good. I then climbed up top of the "igloo," half-thinking I would fall through and land on top of the bear. Taking a good look through the top hole, I could see that there was no bear inside. Jim and Paul looked at each other, obviously confused, so I knew they were not putting me on. They had clearly seen a bear, and they had even mentioned that it had a white patch of fur on its chest, as is common on black bear.

We began searching around the igloo, and we found a decent blood trail leading from the entrance hole. We followed it, thinking now that we were dealing with a wounded bear. After less than a hundred yards, we came upon the bear, stretched out on his belly and stone dead. The arrow had hit an artery, but the thick fat had kept the heavy bleeding inside the body. The bear that my partners had seen was the second bruin, because the dead one had obviously been that way for hours. I am glad that I did not see that second bear, because I may have assumed it to be the one with the arrow in it and blown it away.

We had a good chuckle over the igloo encounter, gutted the bear, and dragged him to where I could drive close by with my junker car. He provided much good eating, along with a good story.

I tried a few more times to hunt these interesting animals, and I killed another a few years later. It strolled right in to the bait, and the only complication this time was getting him to present a decent shot opportunity. He would be broadside one second, and then as I drew, he would shift around and face me. This happened several times, and it was obvious he was hearing or seeing me draw, but he never really seemed to look at me. At last, he stood still when I drew, and the arrow smacked home in the upper, rear lung area. He flinched when the shaft struck him. The nylon string from the tracker, stretched from the launch of the arrow, piled up around the arrow shaft after it came to a stop in the bear's chest. The bear showed no alarm, until he turned his head and spotted the arrow sticking out of him, with fifty feet of dental floss draped around it. He was then gone like a shot, and just like my last victim, he pulled out a bunch of string for a few seconds, and again the string broke. A few seconds later I heard him moan, which they say is a sure sign of a dying bear. That's easy to believe when you are sitting in the kitchen telling tales, but when you turn your back on the brush that the moan comes from and climb down the tree, I can tell you that the doubt is pretty strong.

I sought the help of my neighbor, Bernie Goebel, and we tracked the beast easily from the end of the broken string for twenty yards. In the flashlight beam, I soon saw more string. Obviously, this was the tail end of what was dragging behind the arrow, and I told Bernie as I picked up the end of that second piece of string, "There is a bear at the other end of this." There he was, ten feet away, dead on a bed of sphagnum moss only forty or fifty yards from where I had shot him.

It is interesting to me that bears seem to expire more quickly from arrow wounds than do deer, but with bullet wounds, it seems just the opposite. I have read and been told of many cases where an arrow-struck bear goes right down and dies in a few heartbeats. Neither of the two I killed was very well hit, but they both expired quickly. The second was only hit in one lung and made it only fifty yards. I have seen deer that were hit in one lung, plus the liver, run for great distances before falling. Deer hit by an arrow, even if it pierces both lungs, almost never die without first covering plenty of ground. Perhaps bear do not realize what is going on, consequently not fleeing with the urgency that deer display.

A few days before taking this bear, I had an entertaining evening on stand. I had two active bait stations that season. Near each, I had set up both a shooting stand and a second stand for a camera operator. I wanted to get film of my bear hunt. For the first three evenings of hunting, I had one of my sons along to run the camera. The fourth evening, neither of them was able to come along, and of course, that was when I got my bear. On the third evening stand, though, we had some action that, while not caught on film, will be remembered for a long time by my son, Ben, me, and perhaps a bear as well.

My portable was about ten feet off the ground and was set up with the bait pile ten yards to my left as I sat in the stand. Fifteen feet to my right and about five feet higher, I had built a wooden stand where Ben sat with the camcorder and tripod. He would be able to frame his camera shot in a way that would capture both me, and any bear that might be working the bait. We had been on the stand for just a little while when, to Ben's right, I spotted a large bear, about twenty yards away. As usual, our quarry had slipped in with no noise. I turned to look at Ben, and he was looking around and oblivious to what was going on. I slowly raised my hand and waved, by wiggling my fingers. I got his attention. In slow motion, I pointed to the bear and mouthed the word "BEAR." He got a quizzical look on his face, indicating he did not understand. I pointed again and mouthed "THERE'S A BEAR." He still did not get it. I am not sure what else he thought I might be pointing at and quietly drawing his attention to, but finally he realized what was going on. He looked over just as the bear started to glide in on silent feet.

He was a big brute. My heart was pounding, and I was smiling. My son was getting to see some action. I just might get a shot at a real nice bear. The animal walked right in and began to pass between our stands. This was to my right, so it was not possible for me to get a shot, and the bear was so close to Ben that he couldn't get the tripod mounted camcorder trained on the bear because of the steep angle.

As the bear got to where Ben had walked in to climb the tree, it sniffed at his trail. It walked directly to the base of the tree and sniffed the ground, the base of the tree, and then higher and higher up the tree.

Finally, it just looked straight up. I had been watching the bear, and when it looked up, I shifted my gaze to Ben, who was in his seat, leaning forward, and looking wide-eyed right back down at Mr. Bruin. It was priceless. I wished I were holding the camera right then.

After a moment, the bear moved along and sat down directly behind me, less than fifteen yards away. It sat there a while, then began retracing its route back away from the bait. When it was out of sight, Ben and I grinned at each other.

It was still quite some time until the close of shooting, so we stayed quietly on stand in hopes that this lunker would come back in. I thought I heard him moving around in the brush once or twice, but we did not see him again. As darkness came on, we climbed down. When we got to the ground, we heard the bear go crashing off. He had probably never left the area but was just hanging back, a little too suspicious of our setup. When we got out to our vehicle, we had a good laugh.

One of the more unusual experiences I have had with bears happened at my house. It was late summer and still warm enough to be sleeping with the windows open. Our trashcans were in a wooden rack right under our bedroom window, and in the middle of the night, my wife and I were startled from our sleep by a bruin rummaging in the garbage. The headboard of the bed was right against the wall under the window, so when we were lying down, we were only three feet or so from the bear, with the wall in between. I groggily got up, looked out the window, and could make the bandit out in the dim moonlight. I yelled at him and he left, but before I could get back to sleep, he was back and this time the yelling did not scare him off. I turned on the light, and that did chase him off. Again I tried to get back to sleep but the hungry critter was soon rattling the trash again. Sherilee was not enjoying this at all. I had always told her that people frightened bears and that all you had to do was yell at them and they would leave. This fellow was making her nervous, and she wanted me to use deadly force on him. At first, I didn't really want to, but finally agreed. I went and got a shotgun and some slugs from the gun cabinet, but by the time I got back, the bear had left again. I put the gun on the dresser and doused the light, knowing he would be back. Sure enough, he returned in just a few minutes.

With the light on, I would not have been able to see the bear outside. Without turning it on, I loaded the gun and stood on the bed next to the headboard. My window screen was not removable, so with my wife's permission, I decided to shoot right through it. I could make out the shape of the bear in the darkness, but not well enough to take good aim. When he moved his head in next to the trashcans, everything just looked like a black blob. He would back out every few seconds and swing his head this way and that, and at those times, I could easily make out his shape. I could not see the bead on my gun barrel, but I had shot this gun so often I did not think I needed to. There I was, dressed only in my briefs, standing tiptoe on the bed so I wouldn't shoot the windowsill. I was pointing the gun where I expected the bear's head to be, the next time he swung it out of the trash. I saw the head move into the shadow of the gun barrel and I pulled the trigger.

Shooting inside your bedroom can be hard on the ears. When you then consider the three-foot tongue of flame spouting out of the gun muzzle, it makes for quite an impressive show. Blinded by the flame and ears ringing from the blast, I heard the bear thumping off through the field and then crashing through the brush when he reached the woods. I had missed.

My boys were little shavers when this happened, and they slept through it all. In the morning, I told them that Daddy had missed a bear during the night. I showed them where I was and where the bear was, and they both piped up in chorus, "You MISSED?" I was a little embarrassed, but in retrospect, I am glad I missed.

In about 1995, I discovered a bear den while hunting deer with my rifle. It was far back in the woods behind my father-in-law's place, on an island in a big spruce swamp. I had seen some bear tracks in the inch or so of snow that was covering the ground, and then I spotted another one of those igloo shaped root balls from a wind-tipped tree. On a hunch, I walked over. I saw a hole in the side of it, and bear tracks leading inside. Curiosity overcame good judgement, and I wormed a little way inside with my flashlight showing the way. Sure enough, there was a nice size bear inside. He was sleepy but aware of me, and he moved to the far side of the den and turned his face away as if to say, "Let me sleep." I visited him several more times during that winter, carrying

"I was terrified of them when I was small. I am just a little bit afraid of them now."

Walt Prusi with bear taken in about 1955.

both my camcorder and still camera. The video is poor, for I had no light on the camera and filmed with a flashlight taped to the top of it. The still pictures are clear, but the bear is hiding his face and all you can see is a huge mound of beautiful black fur.

Bears are great game animals, and I enjoy going after them now and again. I get much more satisfaction from taking a whitetail buck than a bear, but if I was more particular in my bear hunting and waited for a bigger animal, it might provide the same challenge. The baiting aspect detracts a little from the pure sportsmanship of bear hunting for me. It's kind of fun to do, and the bears are wising up to it a lot now. Increasingly, they will only visit the bait after dark. They are not quite the suckers for a free handout that they were a few years ago. I think a whitetail buck is still a higher quality trophy, but that is not a putdown on bear. They are great trophies, and hunting them is great fun.

Chapter Nine
Wild Turkey

In 1981, something, or maybe it was someone, told me I should give turkey hunting a try. Minnesota had just begun issuing licenses for spring hunting of the reintroduced flock. I was lucky enough to draw a permit, and that started a long quest for a gobbler. It ended ten years later on an oak-covered ridge near the Whitewater River. It was one of the greatest experiences in all my years of hunting.

I made three unsuccessful trips for turkey. The Minnesota season is structured so that you get a maximum of five days to hunt, and you don't normally draw a permit every year. That kind of limited time makes it tough for a slow learner, like me, to improve his skills very quickly. In addition, if you do not draw for a season or two, simple people, like me, tend to forget what little they learn on previous hunts.

Many a gobbler had soundly thrashed me on those early hunts. I could relate many stories of such defeat, but one of them stands out prominently. I had double-timed it across one of the deep, rugged ravines that traverse the area we hunted, to try to cut off a bird that was traveling the far ridge. The bird was gobbling up a storm as he walked slowly along that far ridge. I did not quite make it to the top of that ridge when his gobble rocked out of the trees, fifty yards away. I had to hunker down where I was. That was on a 45-degree slope, with my feet wedged against one log, downhill from me, and my gun resting on another, just uphill. I was lying prone in between. I was gasping from the climb and my mouth was as dry as cotton. There I lay for a half-hour or more while the bird, just over the crest and out of sight, shook the leaves off the trees with his gobbling. I never got a shot.

I have many such stories. Finally, in 1991, things went a whole lot better.

The first day out that season, I had jumped a gobbler from a field at mid-morning. In talking with a fellow who had hunted the same area a few days before, I found out that he had had the same experience, in the same place, at the same time. Most likely, it was the same bird. I decided that the next day, I would set up in that spot with my decoy and just wait to see if the gobbler showed up. Like deer, turkey will often follow such a routine. I made up my mind that no matter what the temptation, I would sit still there until that hour had passed. I had often seen birds following a schedule for several consecutive days. This was not how I liked to hunt turkeys. This was basically stand hunting, which is great for bow hunting deer, but real turkey hunting is calling them in to your gun. Well, I thought, I need to do what I need to do. I wanted to kill a gobbler. If I had to compromise a little on this first one, so be it. I was in my chosen spot, with my decoy out, well before any hint of dawn.

When dawn came, it brought a beautiful spring day. The wildlife in this area abounds, and every day was a nature lover's dream. Many songbirds and critters were out and about, taking part in the rites of the season. The turkeys began gobbling early, and they gobbled often. Soon, I heard what I was sure was my bird start his morning gobble session. Yelping and clucking with my diaphragm call, I pleaded with him to come over. He was very vocal, and he answered me call for call. He moved from directly to my right, to behind me and to the right, following a ridge where I had hunted many times. The field and decoy were to my left. I reckoned that if I did not bring the bird in with my calling, he would go silent in an hour or two as they usually seemed to, and then feed his way into the field, which is also pretty common. He threw me the first curve when he decided to just work back and forth on the ridge and gobble up a storm, keeping up a steady conversation with my call and me. I knew the odds were good that he would eventually walk into my ambush, calling or not. I started to think that maybe he was suspicious of my calling and that was what was keeping him on the ridge. Then I thought, if he were suspicious, he would leave or at least shut up. Still, I could not stand just sitting there with him challenging me. I picked up and moved towards him.

This Whitewater country is difficult to negotiate, especially for a flatlander from Cedar Valley. I had to cross gullies and rocks, and this was complicated by the fact that there had been recent logging. The resulting debris was thick on the ground. I moved quickly but cautiously, stopping to call now and again, and always he answered. I set up in a couple of different spots, but the bird stuck to the ridge top and one certain area, vocal but not coming in to me. While making one of my moves, I jumped some deer and they crashed off in the direction of the bird, shutting him up for a half-hour or more. Eventually, he started gobbling again, and I moved up a little, sitting on the ground with my back to a big tree. We talked to each other for a long time.

At one point I heard a yelp behind me and to the left, and started cussing my luck because I thought another hunter was moving in. It turned out to be a jake, and he came in along the ridge top just to my left, giving me a heck of a start. I tried to bring the gun around when he passed behind a tree, but he spooked and was gone in a flash, "putting" as he went. I could have snapped a shot but did not, and then I was sorry for it when my big gobbler quit calling. The alarm "putt" of the jake evidently made the big bird more cautious. This was only temporary though, and he started up again shortly. One other time he quit when gunfire erupted—three shots, on a ridge one-half mile away, where my partners were. I hoped that one of them had some luck, and that the luck had not cost me a chance at this bird that I had been working for so long. I was relieved when the gobbling started again after a short period of silence.

This had now gone on for several hours. I was calling less and less, thinking it the wise thing to do. I finally decided not to call anymore at all. The gobbler would sound off only 50 yards away or so, then be quiet, then erupt a hundred fifty yards down the ridge. Soon, he moved back to the nearer location and sounded off again. I waited this out for quite a while, hoping he would come just a little bit closer on one of these return trips, but again he disappointed me. The sun was high in the sky now, and my jangled nerves were starting to really wear on me. I moved again when the gobbler was at the far end of his route. He must have heard something when I moved, because again he was quiet for a time. He resumed gobbling; however, he remained almost stationary, rather than walking back and forth on the ridge.

The position I was in was uncomfortable and still a long way from my adversary. I decided to move in another twenty yards. There, I sat down with my back to a big oak, pulling my feet in towards me and raising my knees to provide a rest for the gun. The shrill gobbling continued, and occasionally I could see red through the brush as the gobbler displayed, strutted, and let the surging hormones and blood color his wattles. It was extremely unnerving.

I had not called for a long time now, and it had not helped or hurt that I could tell. I was nearing the decisive moment. My whole body ached from sitting in awkward, hastily taken positions, and then sitting rock still under high tension. My eyes were watery and getting hard to focus from stretching them through the brush and trying to spot this bird. The adrenaline in my system may have had something to do with it too. I figured I had to do something to break the stalemate, or else

"The battle, waged since before daylight, was over."

The author's 23 3/4 lb. gobbler.

just collapse and die. I got my diaphragm call into my parched mouth, hoping like heck I could make a noise that sounded like a turkey, and gave a couple of very soft yelps. The gobbler started towards me. He didn't gobble or display, he just put his head down and began walking in, stopping every few yards to pick a morsel of food and look around. I picked a marker tree that I judged to be thirty yards away—ideal pattern range for the gun, choke, and loads I was carrying. He stopped a couple of steps from the tree and raised his head to look around. Some light, leafy branches partially obscured him and made the sight picture less than perfect. The branches were not enough to stop the load of copper plated number fours that smacked the big bird down when I touched the trigger.

I leaped to my feet, charged him, tripped on a log, and belly-flopped onto the ground, holding the gun out away from me where I could control the muzzle direction. I scrambled to my feet and sprinted to the bird, which was down and immobilized. In a few seconds, he was deceased. It was 10:30 A.M. The battle, waged since before daylight, was over. I was the winner. How sweet it was.

A twenty-three and three-quarter pound turkey is an armful, but enough of the old adrenaline lingered in my system to get me back to the truck with my bird. My partner, Dan Heikkila, showed up an hour or so later and got to hear the original version of my story. We met Roger and Phil at Red's Roost in Altura, for lunch, and they got the first refined version of the tale.

Roger had a story of his own and a sixteen-pound bird to show off. The three shots I had heard earlier were his. After those shots, I thought I had heard a shout or something, but I was not very sure about that. It turns out that Roger had let out, as Phil put it, "a primordial howl" after downing his bird. It was a very big day for us green-horned, but now blooded, turkey men.

This turkey hunt was about as satisfying as any hunt I have ever experienced. I was one-on-one with a smart, mature bird, and with many opportunities to screw it up. Somehow, I did not.

Chapter Ten
The Yellow Dog

For young hunters and fishermen, there are places, far away, and not so far away, that seem almost mystical. Places that we dream about, and that we long to visit. Such, for me, was the Yellow Dog River. The name itself is special. I cannot think of a better name for a river. By definition, such a place must be difficult to reach, and in places, "the Dog" is exactly that. Mystical places have special inhabitants. Along the fifty-mile course of the Yellow Dog, there are moose, pine marten, wolf, and others of Michigan's rarest creatures. For me, the Yellow Dog's most prominent residents are the native brook trout.

My dad and some of his brothers were addicted to the Yellow Dog and its environs. Their father worked and hunted in the vicinity. I assume that, through him, they were introduced to the area. As a very young boy, Dad was once alone here, for several days. My grandfather kept a team of horses here, for he was under contract to maintain some of the roads. Dad, as young as he was, had been left to tend the horses while his father went home for a holiday break. I loved the woods, but I shivered at the thought of having such an assignment. This was the middle of nowhere when I traveled the country in the 1960's. Dad tended those horses in the 1920's.

Each fall, Dad and I had a special trip that we made. We rose early and loaded our fishing gear, shotguns, and a day's worth of food into the car. Then we spent the day traveling back-roads on our drive to the

Yellow Dog and Huron Rivers. We stopped to hunt grouse along the way, or to fish brookies in the Dog. At the Huron, we fished for salmon, Dad's primary objective. It was a trip we both looked forward to each year. I never remember coming home with much in the way of fish and game. We never did hit it big on the Huron. A few partridge and the odd brook trout were about all I remember us taking. What I most remember is the wild country, the landmarks, and the stories Dad told as we enjoyed our time together.

There were the fire towers, Hairpin and Panorama. Dad had once heard a pack of timber wolves near one of these, the only time he had ever heard the big predators. It had made quite an impression on him. Wolves were extirpated from Michigan about the time Dad introduced me to hunting. The wolves are back now, so the Yellow Dog country has—in a way—been reborn. There was the Mulligan Truck Trail (another wonderful name) and the Triple A Road. There was the Big Pup Creek and its brother the Little Pup, Mulligan Creek, and the Yellow Dog Plains. Dad once pulled over the car in a remote spot, then led me along a faint trail into the woods. We came to a small spring, bubbling out of the ground. There was a dipper, hung on a tree limb, and we used it to take a drink from the spring. The water was cold and crystal clear. The dipper was one of the old, porcelain-coated metal jobs. The porcelain showed rust stains in a few places where water had found its way to the metal. Dad said that the dipper had been there for as long as he could remember. He had walked in, not because he was thirsty, but because he wanted to see if the dipper was still there. Dad had trapped and hunted in this country since he was a young man. When Harry Truman pulled off his upset win in the presidential election, Dad was trapping, living in a tent, in the Yellow Dog country. He was one of the last citizens to be surprised at who his new president was.

The parts of the Dog that I had fished as a boy were wide and rather slow moving. Some of my uncles fished, and I think preferred, the headwaters. I had never fished this portion of the stream, but my Uncle Bill loved the spot. He had taken his son, Chas, to fish the headwaters when Chas was a boy. Years later, Chas found his way back to the very spot where he and his dad had camped on those early trips. He too, grew attached to this stretch of river. His stories about it got me interested in seeing the place, and in seeing that country again. We talked about making a trip there together, and finally did. We have been back a few times since, and never has it been less than wonderful.

The headwaters of this river lie within the boundaries of a federally designated wilderness called the McCormick Tract. The area has an interesting history. Until 1967, the family of Cyrus McCormick, the inventor, owned the tract. When it was willed to the U.S. Forest Service that year, I can remember that it was big news. It had to be big news, for it brought positive comments from my dad, who generally had little to say about the news. There is a story relating to the tract, about an attorney by the name of Richard Bentley. He was an attorney for the McCormick family, and along with them, owned the huge tract. The land is situated near the Huron Mountain Club. The exclusive club was, and is, a retreat for the wealthy. During the years when Bentley was traveling to the compound and club, it was customary to travel to the small town of Champion via the railroad. While there was a road from Champion to the family compound, only forest, swamps, and streams lay between there and the Club. Bentley hired men to clear a trail from the McCormick/Bentley compound, all the way to the Huron Mountain Club.

The trail workers were given specifications. The path was to be wide enough for a man to walk along with his arms outstretched, straight from his sides, without his hands touching any trees or underbrush. There was to be enough overhead clearance to allow a woman, with a parasol, to walk the trail without her umbrella hitting any limbs. Low, wet areas along the trail were to have corduroy put down on them, and all streams would have log bridges built across them. This was the Bentley Trail. It is said that Mr. Bentley made inspections, with umbrella in hand. When I last visited the river, traces of this trail were still visible.

Each time that Chas and I made the trip, we drove to the wilderness boundary, arriving late at night. There, we slept in the box of his pickup truck, sheltered by the topper. In the morning, we prepared our breakfast on a camp stove. We used the truck tailgate for a table. Once we used the tailgate for our plate as well, for in our hasty departure we had neglected to take any plates with us. After breakfast, we hiked for forty-five minutes or so, to reach the river. The walk was through northern hardwood forest, mature maple, oak, and basswood, until we approached the river. Virgin pine and hemlock grew here, along with the biggest cedar trees I have ever seen. There were no sounds of chain saws, or even airplanes. There were only the sounds that we ourselves created, along with those of the birds. We saw, and even used, some of the ancient wooden bridges that Mr. Bentley had kindly provided. We did so with much caution.

The stream is narrow here, and it courses through rocky ravines. There is a beautiful waterfall, the foot of which lies within a rocky chasm. Upstream from this falls were wide beaver meadows, and it was there that we did most of our fishing. Chas is a fly-fisherman, and I used spinning tackle with spinners or night crawlers. Our first trip here together was the most productive, as far as catching fish. Even at that, we did not catch many. Perhaps ten combined. None were bigger than eleven inches, but they were trophies, for they were native brook trout from the wilderness, and from the Yellow Dog. Beautiful to look at, and tasty on the table. To catch them in such a place added to their quality.

To walk to such a place is an adventure in itself, fish, or no fish. This place has meant something to important people in my life. It is a place with beauty and a colorful past. To journey to such a place is to walk with history.

My last such journey took place in the early '90s. Chas and I took our sons along. The fishing was poor, and the boys teased us about our special river. I think they will one day understand, and perhaps they already do, for more than a decade has passed. We enjoyed a picnic that day when we returned to the van after the morning angling adventure. On the ride out, we put the van through its paces, driving it through places that should be reserved for making those "tough pickup truck" ads, where water flies and the truck wheels leave the ground. We saw snow on the ground. The road ran through a deep cut in a rock ledge, and in this shaded canyon some snow still survived. It was July. The rock-cut had been blasted out for a rail line. The road, and our van, traveled where the trains once ran.

"There are places, far away, and not so far away, that seem almost mystical. Such, for me, was the Yellow Dog River."

The headwaters of the Yellow Dog.

When I sat down to record this chapter on the Yellow Dog, I thought I should research the history a bit. When I did, I found some things I expected and some that I had not dreamed of. I thought the area was all virgin timber, but a web site told me that portions of it had been logged or burned over. The portions of Mr. Bentley's trail that I had walked were not the main trail that led to the Huron Mountain Club, but a spur trail used for access to the river and upper falls. I suspected that I might discover such information. It does not disappoint me, for I walked on those rickety, rotting bridges that are credited to Mr. Bentley, and I have photos of Chas and me, standing by the trunks of the huge trees.

I had some reservations about including detailed information on the place where we fished, at the headwaters of the river. I thought Chas would wince at such a disclosure. Then, while doing my web search, I found a site devoted to the Yellow Dog. I was not a little surprised. I was aware that the river was well known, and has been since I was a lad. However, when I read that guided tours are occasionally conducted to the falls, I was flabbergasted!

I cannot help but picture Chas, fishing quietly at the foot of the falls. The sounds of rushing water overwhelming all others. I see him turning around and looking into the smiling faces of two dozen hikers. Yuppies with khaki jackets, old ladies in floppy hats, binoculars around their necks, and Japanese folks armed with multiple cameras. The guide will tell the tourists that it is their lucky day, for they have stumbled onto a rare and endangered species—the woodsman.

The headwaters of the Yellow Dog are now part of the National Wild and Scenic Rivers program, and the McCormick Tract, part of the National Wilderness Protection System. The web site I discovered belongs to a private group whose mission is to protect the entire Yellow Dog watershed. The Dog is special to many. The river and its environs have been afforded both a measure of protection, and a measure of publicity. Such places are both blessed and cursed. The protection ensures that the beauty of the place will not be compromised, and that should please us all. What I fear, is that publicity may strip away what the Yellow Dog has always been—a mystical place, available only to a dedicated few.

Chapter Eleven
Then Came Ducks

It was the third Saturday of October 1995. I was at church services, and the warmth of the crowded room made my face sting. My cheeks were tender from wind, sun, and cold, to which they had been exposed for most of the day. Tim and Jim both smiled when they saw me because they knew I had been up to something. Here I was in church, looking extremely tired, but smiling like a teenager who just got a date with the homecoming queen. That morning, I had had a good duck shoot.

For whatever reason, I did not get into duck hunting until I was in my late thirties. In earlier years, I had tried it a few times, but I had never been all that impressed. True, I had never had a big shoot, but I just did not get all the sentiment of these die-hard waterfowlers. I was having plenty of fun with deer hunting, beagles, and my other outdoor pursuits. I never dreamed that any hunting could be as great as bow hunting. That is, until I started doing wildlife management projects on my property and began watching ducks on the ponds I had built. When the ice went out in the spring, I kept the shallows full of corn for the birds to feed on. I watched them courting and defending the territories they established. I built some blinds and spent hours watching and videotaping the birds. Watching them drop out of the sky with cupped wings and their feet reaching down for the water was awe inspiring, and I began to think that perhaps I should check out this duckin' business. About that time, a friend from work brought me out and showed me his captive flock of ducks. There were woodies, teal, and mergansers. He had raised birds for years awhile back and was getting back into it. I was impressed with the birds.

I had recently purchased a 3-inch chambered 12-bore for turkey hunting. The gun would be a good duck weapon as well, so I had the gun I would need. I had bagged a buck the first week of bow season. One of the stands I had often used during the bow hunt was near a big beaver pond. That pond had become a local duck roost. I had watched the ducks working in and out of this pond each morning and evening. It seemed like it might be a good time to give the sport a try. It was 1991.

The second day of the duck season, which is the first day you can hunt ducks at sunrise in Minnesota, I was at the roost pond. A couple of hundred ducks flew out, but not over me. Lesson One: Scouting pays in duck hunting. The next morning, I was crouched behind the beaver dam where most of the birds had passed over the previous day. At sunrise, the exodus began, and in ten minutes, I had nearly melted down the barrel of that 12-bore. Three birds (the limit that year) were down on the water. I had to wade into the frigid, crotch-deep water to hunt for the birds. I found one easily, another after an hour of bone-numbing wading, and I never found the third. Lesson Two: Waders are good, and a dog would be better. In spite of the tough introduction, the rest, as they say, is history.

As I write this, in May of 2002, my six-year-old golden retriever is curled on the floor next to me. Her name is Jill, and she has been astounding her master for six wonderful duck seasons. To my right, curled up on the bed, is a gangly, five-month old golden retriever named Jake. He is already taller than Jill and will likely outweigh her by thirty pounds when he finally grows into his feet. These feet look to me like they belong on a timber wolf. He has begun his basic training and has recently made his first water retrieve. It has only taken this long because the ice has only recently gone out. My canoe is now painted in a camouflage pattern, and my garage has decoys crammed in every nook and cranny. My den has waterfowl art on the walls, old decoys in the bookshelf, and calls and lanyards slung from the deer racks. You will see membership stickers for waterfowl organizations on the rear windshield of my vehicles. To top it all off, behind the pine trees, and next to the yard, are covered pens. Here, for several years, I kept my own captive flock of waterfowl. Yeah, I got it bad. Tim calls me "father duck".

Be that as it may, the marriage is doing well and the kids are grown and gone. I have time to be a waterfowler, if maybe not the budget. I am hooked, and there is no way to unhook me. It is, the doctor declared, an incurable disease. I am in the advanced stages of it. Life is good.

If you do not know it yet, I am pretty much nuts over nature. Spotting something new or unusual in the outdoors is great fun for me. Well, duck hunting is very conducive to wildlife watching. You hunt ducks in wetlands, which are terrific places to spot critters. In Minnesota, during the first part of duck season, you may only hunt until 4:00 P.M. During that same time of year, bow hunting is much better in the evening hours than it is in the morning. Therefore, you can waterfowl hunt early, when its productive and legal, and only miss the poorer bow hunting hours. Then in the evening, when the deer really move, you can be in your stand. You may as well be in that deer stand, because it is illegal to duck hunt. Duck hunting just fits well with my life and schedule.

Another plus to duckin' is that, unlike deer hunting, you don't have to worry about scent, or keeping immaculate so the game won't smell you. You can rattle around a little and have coffee without blowing the hunt. I have come to enjoy that part of the hunt so much that I find myself going out earlier and earlier as the season progresses. I do that so that I can set up the dekes, have a few cups of swill, a sweet roll, or two, and enjoy the sunrise. At least until its light enough to identify ducks. Few things are more pleasant than watching a pretty sunrise in a duck marsh while you nurse a good cup of coffee and wait for the wonderful sound of wings.

Now that you get the picture of what duck hunting did to me, I will get back to that story of my sleepy evening in church. I could lie and tell you that I paid close attention to every word of the sermon that night, but actually, I think I may have fallen asleep.

That morning, all my planning and studying of this new hobby had come together nicely. I finally had a duck hunt like those you see in the videos. We had been having a wet fall, and the backwaters of the Floodwood River were flooded. Seasonal ponds were now lakes, too deep for the puddle ducks to feed in. Fields and woods were inundated and drawing the ducks from their normal feeding areas. This had thrown me for a loop at first. When I finally realized what was happening, I was able to adjust and I started doing well. This particular day, I decided to try a slough between where the main river and one of its former channels ran parallel to each other, about three hundred feet apart. The slough was surrounded by river maple and oak trees, which were flooded. A day or two earlier, I had jumped a nice flock of mallards out of the timber around this open slough.

As always, I pushed off in the black of night. It was snowing quite hard. The flakes alternating from wet and slushy to hard pellets of ice. A stiff wind put some sting into them when the meandering river took me in an upwind direction. I had a mile or so to paddle, and my gas lantern ran out of fuel within the first two or three minutes. I decided not to use my flashlight full time, figuring I could save the batteries for when and if I got really turned around. I had spent considerable time on this water the last few years, and hoped I could operate in the dark. As it turned out, I had little difficulty. The steady winds actually helped, by constantly letting me know the direction in which I was heading. Only two or three times did I get off course and have to switch on the light, then backtrack a little, and resume my paddle down the old river channel.

When I finally reached my destination, I set up a dozen magnum mallard blocks in the little round opening, plus two or three woody dekes. I pulled the canoe into heavy brush, and as the eastern sky brightened, ever so slightly, I poured myself a hot cup of coffee and munched on a piece of pie. I was enjoying myself immensely. As shooting light grew near, I moved to a position upwind of my blocks and leaned against a big maple tree. The snow was now wet and heavy, and I announced myself with some calls.

Soon the hiss of wings could be heard, and I saw a pair of mallards to the south, winging over the main river. My calling turned them, and they soon spotted my flock of impostors and decided to join them in the little sheltered pool. The wind above the tall trees was tricky for them, and they did the normal mallard thing of setting their wings, then changing their minds and going round again for another pass. On the next pass, they alternately flapped, then braked, with their wings. Just when I was sure they were going to pass over and do another swing, they dropped in on top of me. Cup-winged, spraddle-legged, and teetering on the breeze, they reached their big orange feet down for the water. They were close when I pulled up the gun, and the wind and the momentum hindered their attempt to flare. One bird crumpled at my first shot, but I missed the other as it clawed for altitude right over my head. One down.

Other birds were now on the move, and nearly all of them responded to my calls by at least giving my spread a look. A few ducks answered from the water in the brush, and I began a conversation with the swimmers, trying to coax them in. By looking intently for these birds, I missed some chances at flyers buzzing the decoys. I talked to the ducks that were on the water for quite a while before I decided to try a turkey-hunting tactic. I just shut up in the hopes that they would come looking for me. That is exactly what happened, for as I watched the sky I heard movement behind me, and there were a mallard and black duck swimming in from behind. I swung around, stepped from behind the tree, and managed to splash both birds when they flushed. This was my first black duck. I picked up my three birds and brought them to the canoe, stopping to pour myself a cup of coffee. As I fiddled with the thermos, a half-dozen birds came in to the dekes, and I shot at long range without hitting anything. Had I been in my normal shooting spot, it would have been a good shooting opportunity. I hid the canoe a little deeper in the brush and moved back to my tree.

Quite a few mallards were on the move, and everything that came by gave us a look. After several flares, I noticed the decoys were covered with snow and I waded out to clean them off. As the morning went on, I had to do this several times. When the blocks were not snow covered, the birds were interested.

A pair came in. I missed the drake at point-blank range, but downed the hen. She was still alive and I shot again as she swam into the willows twenty yards away on the other side of the pool. I splashed after her, and as I was searching, five more birds came in to the blocks. They flared when they saw me. The closest drake was still at extreme range, but I crumpled him. He rocketed down, smacking into a tree, decapitating himself, and splashed down five feet from my maple tree backrest. I returned there, and took up my watch once more.

That was how the morning went. When I quit, there were four big ducks lined up on the canoe seat, and I had lost two others. Two inches of wet snow covered the canoe, and everything was soaked and snow-covered. The snow and wind stopped, and the clouds thinned as I began my paddle out. The exercise warmed me up, the day brightened, and it was beautiful paddling on the still water amongst the snow-whitened hardwoods. It was a chore to drag all the soaking wet gear and the canoe out to the truck. Then it still had to be loaded, and everything was soaking wet and heavy. After the short drive home, it had to be stowed in the garage. A light heart took the pain out of the work. I then had to do some chores, shower, and get ready for church. I slept very soundly that night. I usually do in the fall.

That day on the river was the first really productive decoy shoot I ever had. Several seasons of learning the ropes had begun to pay off, and I had been decoying more and more birds. During this hunt, almost everything was interested in my spread, and enough birds were flying to give me many chances. It was my last good day of duckin' for the season. The birds were leaving. The following weekend, I was back in the same area and saw only one pair of birds. I had caught them the previous weekend during their last days in the area. Some day I will catch them there again. I can't wait.

My duck hunting is a little different from what most people are familiar with. Most people hunt big lakes or big marshes. I love to jump shoot the local beaver ponds and smaller rivers. This is in keeping with my personal preference of being off by myself when I hunt. Seldom, if ever, do I encounter another hunter. Hunting these areas keeps you from seeing as many ducks as other people do, but with limits as low as they are today, you often don't need to see many birds to get your quota. I typically set up my decoys and sit over them for the first morning flights, then paddle or hike around, trying to jump birds. I have a number of quiet, out of the way places where I spend many enjoyable hours. I have now become one of those duck hunting fools that, only a few years ago, were such a great mystery to me.

"Smiling like a teenager who just got a date with the homecoming queen... I had had a good duck shoot."

The dream limit, all greenheads.

Chapter Twelve
The Arkansas Grand Prairie

Every duck hunter who has read about the sport, or discussed it with fellow waterfowlers, knows that one of the great centers of American duck shooting is Stuttgart, Arkansas. Here the Arkansas, White, and Mississippi rivers join. In the fall and winter, the timbered bottoms of these rivers, and the smaller streams that feed them, flood their banks and attract mallards and wood ducks by the hundreds of thousands. Away from the bottoms, there are fertile fields of rice, beans, wheat, cotton, and corn. Many of these fields are also flooded, and it is a paradise for waterfowl.

In 1997, while I was in the bird business, I happened to sell a black duck to a taxidermist from Arkansas. We started chatting about duck hunting. He offered to show me some hot spots and take me out duckin' if I ever got down that way. My curiosity was piqued. I called the Arkansas Game and Fish people and found that the season lasted until January 19. A five-day, non-resident license was only fifty bucks; in addition, a seven-dollar waterfowl stamp was required for duck hunting. This information got me even more interested, and with the duck season in Minnesota two months past, I was ready to get out on the water again. Over the holidays, I casually mentioned the idea of a trip south for a hunt, to my sweet wife. Out of the blue, she said, "Lets go!" This pretty much floored me, but she explained that she was ready to escape the cold and would love to take a little vacation trip with me. Well, that was all it took to get me into serious planning for this trip.

I was able to arrange time off with short notice, and we contacted some friends, who were living in Arkansas. We would plan to do some socializing in addition to my hunting. We contacted Bob and Judy Juola from Hazen (about 20 miles from Stuttgart). Bob went to school with Sherilee, and we know his folks well. Judy also grew up in our area. They invited us to stay with them, and Bob said Judy had a cousin, from Hazen, who was an avid duck hunter. He would talk to this fellow to see about getting me some help finding spots to hunt.

Our trip down was made at a leisurely pace, with overnight stops along the way. We started seeing geese around Kansas City, and spotted a flock of turkey in a cornfield. We stayed one night with friends in northwest Arkansas, and there we saw hundreds of ducks and geese in the rivers and reservoirs. As we neared Hazen and Stuttgart, we saw thousands of geese in the air and on the fields. It was Sunday, the twelfth, when we got to the Juola's. There, we began to experience true southern hospitality. Judy gave us each a call lanyard with a floating camo sleeve on them. A woman she worked with made and sold these lanyards. When the woman heard that Judy had friends from the north who were coming down for duck hunting, she gave them to Judy to pass on to us. Judy said her boss was trying to rearrange his schedule to take me out on a hunt, and that her cousin, Philip, was coming over to give me the scoop on where to hunt as well.

Philip arrived and I found him to be a hunter's hunter and a kindred spirit. He offered me the use of his boat and motor if I needed it, but said that in the morning, all I needed was my gun and shells. He had arranged for Mr. Jerry Carter to take me hunting on my first day. Mr. Jerry was about 60 years old, the former mayor of Hazen, and a bit of a local celebrity. He farms minnows for the bait and aquarium markets, and has taught many of the local lads (including Philip) about duck hunting. Philip advised me to leave my dog home, as the cold and ice conditions were such that the locals preferred to hunt without their dogs. He said to be courteous to Mr. Jerry and do as I was asked, and that I would have a good time. I was told that Mr. Jerry was a deadly shot and an expert caller who knew how to find and bag ducks. Ducks, by the way, to Mr. Jerry and Philip, come in two varieties: Greenhead mallards and scrap ducks. I was to meet Mr. Jerry at Carol's Kitchen, a local restaurant, at five the next morning.

The alarm went off at 4:00 A.M. and I jumped out of bed like a kid at Christmas. I ate a couple of pop tarts, filled my thermos with coffee, then headed to Carol's. It was mean cold, 13 degrees above zero. When I got to Carol's, it looked to be closed until I peeked inside and saw a fellow, about my age, drinking coffee. His camo hat and the duck calls around his neck identified him as a fellow duck hunter, and the lanyard, being nearly full of bands, showed him to be experienced and competent. I went in and asked the fellow if he was hunting with Mr. Jerry Carter and he said yes, so I introduced myself as the Minnesota fellow that was tagging along that day.

His name was Steve, and he was Mr. Jerry's regular companion. Steve told me to help myself to coffee, as there would be no help from the restaurant staff for an hour or so. Evidently the local duck hunters opened the place up each day and got the coffeepots going. Steve said Mr. Jerry and a fellow named Chuck would join us shortly, along with several other local fellows on their way to work. When the others arrived we exchanged pleasant introductions and small talk, mostly centered on why anyone would choose to live in Minnesota during the winter, and what kind of hunting we had up there. After several cups of coffee, we went out, and I loaded my gear into Mr. Jerry's sixteen-foot duck boat. Like nearly all the locally owned boats I saw, the gunwales were reinforced with one-quarter inch thick angle iron to take the punishment dished out by trees as they negotiated the flooded timber.

I had been set up to hunt with some top quality guides. Steve had guided professionally for fifteen years, and both he and Mr. Jerry were guides for some of the hunts sponsored by Waterfowl USA. Steve kept a log of the birds his party bagged each day. Some days it was just he and Mr. Jerry, some days it was as many as six or seven hunters, and the yearly totals were usually 800 to 1,000 birds. This year, the count was way down... about 250 going into the final week of the season. I could not believe my good fortune to have been set up with a couple of hunters like these two fellows.

We drove about eight miles to a boat landing in the Wattensaw

Wildlife Management Area, and broke ice to launch the boats. We were within sight of the White River, on one of its flooded tributaries. Steve had a fuel line problem, and we fooled with it for thirty minutes before getting underway. We then motored upstream for ten minutes or so until we found some reflective markers on the trees. We followed these for a couple of hundred yards off of the main channel, breaking inch thick ice in spots, until we arrived at a natural opening in the timber, surrounded by buckbrush. There, we rigged a dozen decoys on a single long cord with one end tied to a springy branch. The other end was in Steve's boat, and he and Chuck would jerk the cord to give movement to the decoys. I had never seen mallard blocks rigged this way, but Mr. Jerry explained that the movement and the calling were the important items, rather than the placement of the blocks. It was starting to get light as we pulled the boats into the buckbrush to hide and ducks were beginning to whiz overhead. It would be an understatement to say I was keyed up.

Wood ducks and mallards passed over and around us. There were birds in sight almost constantly. My guides said that this was a poor morning flight, but it was better than almost any I had seen back home. Few birds passed close to us, but Chuck, Steve, and I all missed a couple of shots at wood ducks. After an hour, we moved the boats and blocks a little, and shortly thereafter, Chuck nailed a decoying woody drake. Then a small, dark duck decoyed and I shot twice, folding him up with the second shot. It was a lesser scaup drake. After a two-month layoff, I had bagged a duck.

Steve and Chuck decided to pull out and get the motor repaired, leaving Mr. Jerry and I alone at the decoy spread. I was enjoying getting to know my guide, and really enjoying being out duck hunting again. At one point, I had tried to join in and help with the calling. Mr. Jerry said I would probably have better luck if I took the reed out of my call! I took the hint and lay off my mallard call, though I still squealed my woody call now and again and got a few birds interested. Then, as I turned to talk to Mr. Jerry, a pair of wood ducks decoyed. I dropped the drake with my first shot, slowed the hen with my second, and missed her clean with my third. I was pleased, but I asked Mr. Jerry if I was offending anyone by shooting at scrap ducks. He said no, it was pretty hard to offend him and his partners. We went back to visiting and comparing notes on hunting, religion, politics, and what have you. Then a flock of eight or so ducks decoyed from my left, and as I pulled up, they flared. I saw green heads and dropped a still descending bird with my first shot. As the birds rocketed up, I dropped another in the decoys, and then as they gained speed and altitude I realized it was a flock of shovellers as I shot the third time and dropped a third bird. A clean triple, the first I have ever shot.

Mr. Jerry didn't say much, but I figured he had to be impressed with the triple. Mr. Jerry had hardly raised his gun and seemed content to do the calling and instruction that his Yankee newcomer needed. I had my five-bird limit on our first morning out.

We stayed another hour or so, sharing coffee from my thermos and good conversation. Then we cut loose our decoys, picked up the birds, and motored out to the channel. When we got there the sky was full of high-flying flocks of mallards, thousands of birds winging to or from their feeding areas. We set up again in another opening for a little while but had no shots, then called it a morning and headed back to town. I had my five birds and was happy, but Mr. Jerry said it was a poor flight, especially because we got only one or two cracks at mallards. He also said it was unusual to see anything but mallards or woodies in the timber, but that the cold weather had frozen many of the fields and chased the scrap ducks into the timber.

Back at Bob's, I rested for a while. I had to keep pinching myself to make sure it was not all a dream: shooting Arkansas's flooded timber with a pleasant, capable companion who seemed to want me to do all the shooting. I had a wonderful five days of Arkansas duckin'.

One evening, Mr. Jerry brought me to hunt at his private lake. We drove through some crop and pastureland, and put in the boat at a large, open pool surrounded by thick-based Cyprus trees. The lake was now connected to the White River due to the floodwaters, and we crossed the open area and entered the timber, threading our way through the oaks and beech and maple. We jumped several dozen mallards and pulled the boat into some brush near a twenty-yard wide opening in the timber. I was dumbstruck, as for fifteen minutes the air above us had from thirty to a hundred fifty mallards in sight at any one time, all headed in the same direction. Mr. Jerry motored over in the direction they were headed, and we jumped about three hundred birds from one area. We stopped the boat and Mr. Jerry started to call, complaining at the small number of birds about. He says in a typical year there are birds in sight at all times.

I still had not killed a mallard, but shortly a pair came over, quite high. I took a shot at the greenhead and dropped him. He recovered and began to flutter away and I had to twist and shoot behind me to anchor him. These were two tough shots, but I hit both and Mr. Jerry complimented me. I missed a couple of pass shots, then dropped a second greenhead. He needed some finishing off on the water. It was starting to get dark now, and the mallards were flying to roost. Mr. Jerry worked his call constantly. Hundreds of birds flew over in marginal range, and it was tough shooting through the canopy. I missed at least ten shots before finally tagging another big greenhead as shooting hours came to a close.

I believe Mr. Jerry took a couple of shots that outing. I should tell you about the shotgun he shoots. It is a Valmet over and under… 36 inch barrels, both full-choked, and light as a feather. He loves that gun. Philip claims to have seen him kill mallards at a hundred yards with it. Even if Phil is off by thirty yards, that is impressive shooting.

Back at the landing, we went and got the truck good and stuck, and had to unhook the boat and trailer while they were still in the lake. It took an hour to get the truck out, and then we had to drive to the little town of Bisco to get a rope to pull out the trailer and boat. I got a big hug from Mr. Jerry when we got the rig out.

Mr. Jerry's truck made quite an impression on me. I think it was a GMC, or maybe a Chevrolet, but that was not the most significant thing about it. It was dirty and rusty. There were toolboxes at the front of the box and along the sides. I never got a good look inside the toolboxes, but I imagined they would hold a cluttered assortment like the pickup box did. Only, the items would be smaller. The box of the truck contained a couple of acetylene tanks, plastic buckets, life jackets, minnow nets, jumper cables, various loose tools, and a general collection of farm related paraphernalia. Inside, the cab was just as cluttered. The dashboard was dusty and grimy. There was a beverage holder stuck on the dash and it usually had a plastic bottle of Mountain Dew rattling around inside it. A large, half-full bottle of Tums lay wedged between the beverage holder and the cracked windshield. A Ruger semi-automatic .22 pistol dangled in a holster from the steering column. Mr. Jerry's parka, two boat cushions, and his beloved Valmet shotgun always rode in the cab. All of this was piled on the seat, between us, and spilling onto the floor. Beneath these was a carton of the little orange restaurant crackers, the kind that are in the little cellophane packs of four or five one by two-inch crackers. Mr. Jerry was constantly nibbling on these crackers and taking hits on the Mountain Dew bottle. The dash also held some type of bound booklet of forms. Perhaps it was a ledger. There was a CB radio, to boot. It was a truck that was obviously used a lot. It looked to me like it was Mr. Jerry's mobile headquarters. I liked it because it made my truck seem clean.

Back at Bob and Judy's we had a good visit, and I hit the sack tired and happy. As I closed my eyes to sleep, I could see mallards in the tree tops, cupped winged and dropping in to land. It was beautiful to fall asleep with those visions.

I was on my own on the third day. I decided to take my canoe and head out to the same area that Mr. Jerry and I had hunted on my first day of the trip. This plan died early when I took a wrong turn in the dark and buried my car in a mud hole. Some duck hunters gave Jill and me a lift to the hunting area, and they showed me a spot where they had seen a duck hunter on foot with a lab. They dropped me off there, and I made my way downhill until I hit flooded timber. There, I sat down to see what might fly over. The day was a lot warmer, perhaps 30 degrees, but the ice was still on the shallow flooded area. As the sun started to rise, I heard the familiar squeal of wood ducks leaving the roost, and soon I shot at one passing over and knocked it out of the sky. It bounced off the ice nearby, and Jill got to do her first duck retrieve in a couple of months. It was a hen woody. I missed a few more shots, and as the morning exit flight petered out, I followed the edge of the flood to see what I might find. I happened onto a beaver flooding and took up position on the edge of it. It was drizzling on and off, and the ice on the pond was beginning to rot away, although it was still thick enough to hold up Jill.

I followed the edge of the pond, stopping now and again to watch the sky. Not many birds were flying, but at one point, a pair of mallards began to circle the pond. I hid behind a big oak tree. They came into decent range and I hit the drake with my second shot. He bounced off the ice fifty yards away. Jill did not see the bird fall and after a bit of screwing around I managed to direct her to the bird, with hand signals. She had to break some ice and did not like the tough going, but eventually my haranguing convinced her to retrieve the beautiful big greenhead.

I poked around for another hour without jumping any birds and saw few that were flying low enough to be considered workable. On the way back, I walked out onto one of the dams and sat halfway across it for a time. Jill caught a nutria out on the ice, and it was a comical chase for a minute or two as she spun her wheels for traction, as did her adversary. The rodent would flee until Jill nearly caught it, then turn to fight. Much slipping and sliding accompanied each stop and start, and it was a funny sight. I called her off to avoid anyone getting hurt.

I sat on the dam for another half-hour, and soon wood ducks began to fly about. Many of them were low enough to give me a shot if only they came near. I missed a couple of shots, then called in a bunch of six, and had them setting their wings. They spotted the dog—or me— and flared overhead. My shot folded a nice drake and he crashed into the ice below the dam. Jill retrieved him for me, and I headed back to the road with my three ducks. It was raining hard and steady by now, and I started to get soaked through my rain gear. I still had to get my car out, but I could not help but explore a little. By the time I got back to the road I was soaked and tired. A passing hunter gave me a ride to my car, and a couple of squirrel hunters with a four-wheel drive pulled me out. I got back to our motel room and a very worried Mrs. Prusi, about two o'clock. The hunt was three days gone and I had killed twelve ducks.

I had nothing set up for the following day and planned to go back to the beaver pond with some decoys, but in the evening Philip called and said Mr. Jerry wanted to take me out again. That being the case, I was again at Carol's Kitchen at 5:00 A.M., and Mr. Jerry and I drove to the Bayou Meto, south of Stuttgart. The boat landing had 75 to 100 vehicles there. We launched the boat and idled up the bayou, looking for birds and a place to set up. Mr. Jerry did not like what he saw, and decided to move to a different landing. This we did, and again motored around looking for working birds and a place to set up. The bayou was full of hunters, and the iced-in shallows made it hard to get back into areas and be by yourself. Mr. Jerry kept moving and stopping, looking around for birds and open spots. We saw many crippled ducks on the water, and could have filled our limits with them. After a while, Mr. Jerry realized we were nearly out of gas. He had hefted the tank earlier and it felt full because it was frozen to the bottom of the boat! We headed out to the landing and ran out of fuel. Some duck hunters from Alabama towed us out and then sold us some gas.

All morning, guns had been pounding away as thousands of mallards, and hundreds of wood ducks, filled the sky. Now, at the landing, many of the vehicles were gone as their owners had filled their limits or otherwise called it quits. I was a little disappointed, because we had not really set up to shoot yet, and the day was several hours gone. Now, said Mr. Jerry, we were ready to duck hunt, and off we went up the bayou.

We set up a couple of hundred yards off the channel, and Mr. Jerry began to work his call. Many birds were overhead just out of range, and many appeared to be looking for places to land. Mr. Jerry moved us a couple of times, and I had missed a shot or two, when finally he stopped in a spot that seemed to satisfy him. It was probably about ten o'clock. The Arkansas public hunting areas only allow hunting until noon... only two hours left! Now Mr. Jerry went to work with his call, and many birds circled and looked us over. It was windy and the birds were obviously struggling with the wind. Finally, a group of four or five birds passed downwind of us, turned upwind, and set their wings. As they disappeared behind a big tree next to me, I raised the gun. They appeared from behind the tree with crooked, set wings, and with their orange feet reaching down for the water. They turned nearly straight towards me and it was almost too easy. The lead bird spotted me and was just starting to flap its wings for altitude when I hammered it down. The others punched the accelerator and rocketed up in front of me. My second shot nailed a big drake, but he was still airborne and passed over my head. I shot at him again, and I'm not sure if I hit him

Philip Boothe watches the sky from an Arkansas rice levee.

but he came down. Mr. Jerry finished him on the water and I had a nice double.

We continued to work birds, and a big greenhead passed over just upwind... fast and high but in range. I folded him up. He crashed into the upper branches of a tree and hung up there for five seconds until the flapping of his wings broke him loose and he splashed down ten yards off. His head was up so I finished him on the water. Mr. Jerry said, "Naaas shot Dayun.... you lucky sunnuva beech," and we both had a laugh.

Another pair of birds came in—exactly like those that gave me the double—and I missed the greenhead once but dropped him with my second shot. This one took several shots on the water to finish. Now, Mr. Jerry was interested in shooting, and twice missed both barrels on high overhead shots. A pair came into us from his end of the boat. I was looking right over his shoulder at the pair, braking and banking as they came in to land. About fifteen yards out, perhaps less, they saw us. They turned to my left, attempting to grab more sky. I had a beautiful view of the whole thing... sun shining off the birds and Mr. Jerry taking his sweet time getting on the birds. He dropped the drake stone dead. It was about ten minutes to twelve.

Birds were still passing over, and I still needed one to fill my limit. I had my four mallards. Fate was kind, though, and with a couple of minute's left to shoot, I heard the squeal of woodies. A pair came in from downwind. They turned to my left, and it was a tough shot but I touched off as I lost sight of the drake going into the brush. I continued my swing and shot again, totally on timing, and guessing where the bird would emerge from cover. The second shot was a waste, as the bird splashed in dead just as I shot. It was noon. My drake woody, three drake mallards, plus one hen made a nice colorful pile of ducks in the boat. Mr. Jerry and I were a pair of tired hunters by the time we got back to Hazen. We parted with smiles and a handshake. My Arkansas duck hunt was over.

I have made the trip to the Grand Prairie five times now, missing only one year since that first trip. Bob and Judy have become close friends, as has Phillip. The hospitality they have shown us is second to none, and we have come to enjoy the people of the south. With people like this and duck hunting like I have here each trip, I expect I will be making many more trips to Hazen, Arkansas.

Chapter Thirteen
Blood Trail

If there is anything my buddies and I really like to do, as a team, it's blood trailing. After twenty years of working on this skill, we have gotten good at it. In fact, I am convinced that if we had another crack at some of the deer we lost in the early years, we would recover most of them. If you are a bow hunter, you have an obligation to develop this skill, because in spite of what many archery people try not to mention, bow hunting cripples many deer. Because the number of bow hunters is low, this is not really having a detrimental effect on deer herds, but a sportsman owes it to the animal and to the sport to make every effort to retrieve wounded game. I also believe that because of the much higher number of rifle hunters, we lose many more cripples from the gun season than the bow season. All that being said, it does not change the fact that losing a cripple is about the most unpleasant thing that can happen to the bowman. It is much more common than most of the outdoor magazines or books will admit. It is just an unpleasant fact. My dad was somewhat anti-archery hunting because he thought too many deer died without being recovered.

I can't tell you anything based on scientific research; I can only relate my personal experience with deer that my partners and I have hit. I personally have put arrows into 24 big game animals—22 deer and two bear. You already know that I recovered the two bears. I also recovered 18 of the deer. Of the four I did not get, I know one of them recovered. Another would have, but a friend got him with his rifle a week after I winged him. One, I am quite sure, died, and the fourth probably died as well. My guess is that my recovery percentage is better than most. But that has been helped by the fact that I have hit several of my deer in the spine, putting them down immediately. I also walked right up to two others by sheer luck before I even started to really look for them. This is not bragging. Spine shots are poorly executed shots, guided by luck, and I have had four or five of these. I just want to let you know what it is like in the real world of bow hunting. The others took some tracking, some of it very difficult. The biggest factor in what I consider a good recovery percentage, has been the willing and able people who have helped me do the blood trailing.

I beat myself up pretty bad over the first couple of deer I lost, both in 1978, which was my second year of bow hunting. I came close to giving up the bow. I know a few people who did bunch it because of their concerns over crippling. I thought seriously about it in '78, until late in that season when I had one of those close encounters of the deer kind, almost getting a shot but not quite. I realized then that I was hooked, and would not give it up even if I crippled the occasional deer. Hunting with bow is just too darn great an experience. I just applied myself to learning the art of blood trailing, as did my friends, and we have done okay. Here are a couple of examples.

I was bow hunting east of my home on a powerline right-of-way where I had a portable stand attached to a huge balsam tree. This area had always seen heavy deer traffic, and a few years before I had killed my best archery buck close to where this stand was now set up. I had seen a small "rack" buck in this area before the season began and at least one time from this stand when he crossed the power-line, upwind and out of range. He was the buck I was after.

I was taking my evening watch, and it was raining a little when I got into the stand. The buck I was after showed up near the stand well before sunset, but he was to my right where I could not turn easily to get a shot. I stood up in the stand and began turning around to face the tree, which would allow me to shoot to the side where the buck was feeding. As I did this, I had to slide the loop of my safety belt extension along the part of the belt that was around my waist, for it was not long enough to let me turn around without doing so. As I did this, I made a noise. The buck spooked, and jumped back into the brush. After a few minutes, he returned, but he was much more alert. He looked around and sniffed the air constantly. It took a long time for him to calm down, and I did not want to shoot, or even draw, until he did.

After several minutes, he again began to feed, and I drew my arrow back. He was quartering slightly towards me, and just as I got the sight pin where I wanted it and was ready to release, I brushed something with my elbow. The buck's head shot up and he looked right at me. I released the arrow just as he appeared to lock his eyes on me. He jumped the string bad, and as a result, I hit him too far back. (Jumping the string, by the way, is when the target animal reacts radically to the sound of the arrow being released.) The deer sped across, and then along, the powerline. He then slowed to a walk and moved slowly into the woods. His posture indicated that he was badly hurt, his body somewhat hunched up. This "hunching up" often indicates a liver hit. From what I had seen of the arrow's position, that made sense. The arrow entered at a forward ranging angle, and I thought the chances were good that I had hit the lung on the far side. While the deer had been quartering towards me when I released, he had probably turned ninety degrees by the time the arrow hit, so it had hit far back, with that forward ranging angle.

As usual, I headed for home to call for assistance. I was concerned that the drizzle might develop into rain and wash out the blood trail. I called the big three of tracking, Phil, Tim, and Jim. It was a weeknight, and all of these guys live an hour or so from me. The fact that all three of them dropped what they were doing, and came over to track, speaks volumes as to why I like hunting with this bunch.

Because I thought we might possibly have a deer that was gut shot, we waited a couple of hours before starting on the trail. We planned to start tracking and see what developed. If it looked like a lung and liver hit, we would keep after him. If we thought it was gut hit, we would back off and wait some more. In addition to the four of us already mentioned, my son, Ben, came along to help.

The trail was easy to follow where the deer had entered the woods after leaving the powerline right-of-way. We saw the unmistakable evidence of a lung hit, pink frothy blood. We also saw very dark blood that can indicate a liver hit, and before long, a small piece of liver along the trail, verified this. I thought the chances of finding him soon were good, so we kept on the trail. Liver shots are funny though. We have had liver shot deer that dropped before traveling fifty yards, falling before making it off the field where they had been hit. We have also had them cover considerable distance, and live through the night so that we had to finish them off the following morning. I imagine the liver has concentrations of blood vessels inside of it that, if hit, bring death much more quickly than if another part of the organ is hit. Whatever the reason, liver hits are sure kills. It is just a matter of how long it takes, how far they go, and how good you are at staying with them.

The trail of blood left behind by a wounded animal can vary greatly. Some mortal wounds bleed heavily inside the animal and little blood is left along the animal's trail. Some flesh wounds, such as some leg wounds, leave a relatively heavy trail of blood on the ground, but the deer is in no danger of succumbing to the wound. The hunter on the trail of a wounded animal may be able to walk along at a normal pace and see huge spatters of blood every few feet. He may also search on his hands and knees, finding tiny flecks of blood separated by several yards. If you imagine this taking place in the dark of night, you will get an idea of what the hunter is up against.

Tracking went as it typically does, for an hour or so. Easy tracking, then a tough check, then some challenging trailing. It kept getting trickier after that first hour. Shortly, we were on our hands and knees, spread out, following any likely deer trail, just hoping to find spoor. The foliage was drippy from the earlier rains, though now the skies were clear. We were at one check a very long time when I found a drop of pink-tinted water, clinging to a blade of grass. A short distance away, we found more pink drops, and then finally, something that really looked like blood. We were on the track again, though very slowly.

The deer looped back on himself. When he reversed directions, he moved along about forty to fifty yards from, and parallel to, his back trail. There he had bedded, apparently with the intention of being able to monitor his trail to see if we were tracking. It was where he made the long sweeping turn as he doubled back that we had the worst time on the trail, but we succeeded in staying on it.

It was getting late, so I hiked out to the fields with Ben to get him started towards home. He had school in the morning so he was excused from the remaining fun for the evening. When I returned to the tracking party, I saw a scene that I will never forget, just because it was so surreal looking. It felt like I was watching a movie. The woods were wet, and obviously so were we. The activity of moving around had us very warm. The night was clear now, but the heavy moisture in the air and on the foliage was raising a ground fog. There were my three pals, standing in a circle with a gas lantern in the center. They were hunched over, looking for sign. Depending on where each stood, relative to the lantern, each was either illuminated or silhouetted by its light. Steam was rising off them and off the lantern, and the whole scene was shrouded in the ground fog. Partner, it was spooky looking. I flattened the raised hair on the back of my neck and joined them to resume the quest.

From his bed, the deer had obviously heard, and most likely seen us, moving along his trail. He abandoned the bed. Often, after a wounded deer has bedded and then gotten up again, the blood sign gets thinner. Time and lack of movement allows clotting of the wound to take place. Fortunately for us, it worked just the opposite this time. From the bed, the blood was steady, although in small quantity. It took good tracking to stay with it but we had only short periods where we were not making progress along the trail. We were tiring now, though, and the late hour and fatigue from several hours of tracking would soon begin to rob us of our effectiveness. We took a breather to rest our eyes, backs, and legs and had a high old time teasing each other. We laughed at our situation and ourselves. Phil was a snuff user and I bummed a pinch from him, saying it would affect me as spinach does Popeye. After a ten-minute breather, we pushed on.

The snuff did it. After the break, it was just five or ten minutes of moving steadily along the track before we found him. He was dead, and appeared to have died on his feet. The arrow had entered the gut area, pierced the liver and one lung, and narrowly missed the heart. It was sticking out six inches on the exit side. Jim had a camera along and took some photos that he later gave to me. You should see me grinning in those photos. When we got back to the house, I set up the camcorder. The video is funny to watch. It is two in the morning and we are all pretty giddy and showing off for the camera. The buck was just a 7-point, but the efforts that went into bringing him in turned him into a trophy. In fact, you might say that the pursuit of this buck took over a year. My son, Danny, and I had both missed this buck the previous season. The shape of the rack was distinctive, and I recognized him.

The fourth deer I killed with archery tackle also led us on quite a chase. She had been quartering slightly towards me when I shot. She jumped the string, trying to spin away from me when she heard the twang. The arrow hit her in a back leg and knocked her right down for just a second, then she raced off. I summoned Tim and Roger to help track.

It was one of those cold, clear autumn nights with abundant stars and no moon. The country where this big doe led us was low, swampy cover that straddled a small stream. There was a lot of low, willow brush and alder, with deer trails crisscrossing everywhere. It was tough going for us with the brush. We had good blood sign to begin with, and several times we heard deer move off ahead of us. This area was really attracting deer that year, so it may or may not have been our wounded doe. Several times, Tim and Roger were sure they smelled the deer, and they may well have.

We had tracked for perhaps an hour when the deer crossed the little stream. Roger and I stayed on the spot where she had entered the water, while Tim headed out to the state highway, a quarter-mile off, to cross the stream via the road. When he arrived opposite the bank from us, we then followed his route to join him. It was just a little chilly to be swimming. Fortunately, the deer did not swim the stream again after that, or she would have worn us out quickly.

It seemed as though the swim had stopped the blood flow quite dramatically. Our progress became slower and slower. We heard owls and we heard coyotes and it was a beautiful night to be in the woods.

At one point, we gave up, intending to come back in the morning. We headed for some fields near our location in order to have some easy walking back to the road and then to our vehicles. While on the way out, we happened to notice some blood on one of the tractor trails that connected two of the fields. We attempted to follow this, but made little further progress. We bunched it for the night.

Those nights, when I have left an animal in the woods to wait for daylight, were the longest, most restless nights I had experienced since the Christmas Eves I suffered through as a boy. Exercise right before bedtime will keep you awake; in addition, you are anxious to get back on the trail and worried about finding your animal. When sleep would finally come to me, I would dream about the deer and that I was trailing it again. Naturally, if you have left the trail for the night, you have one of the tougher tracking jobs on your hands. The thought of losing the animal makes you sick. As always, that night was a long and restless one.

Roger had spent the night at my place, but Tim had returned to the tent camp. He was to return in the morning with more of the group. We planned to put hunters on stand while the others tracked. Roger and I did not wait, but headed out at first light. He had his bow but I left mine behind rather than have to fight that thick brush with it again. We needed a weapon though, because we expected to find the deer alive.

When we got to the point where we had quit trailing the previous evening, we found that after losing the trail the previous night and stumbling on it again, we had tracked it in the wrong direction. There were so many deer tracks in that particular spot that we never realized our error. That is, until we got back that morning. We were able to track steadily, but not very quickly. The trail led us across a bit of an island in the swamp. It was covered with large aspen with thick brush beneath that. There were several such islands, surrounded by open areas that had only long, swamp-grass growing in them. We got to the edge of the island, and when I looked across the hay to the next island, I saw the head of a deer staring at us. I could tell that it was a yearling. I thought it likely that this was the young deer that accompanied my wounded doe. It did not dash off, so we thought that the doe was likely bedded right near her yearling. We made a plan, and Roger circled back and around to another spot where there was a good deer crossing. I would follow the trail and hope that the doe moved past Roger so that he could get another arrow into her.

The yearling fled when I crossed the hay swamp, and I continued tracking. Just a minute or two after I got onto the next island, I heard crashing in the brush thirty yards ahead. As I listened, I realized that the sound was not typical of a fleeing deer. It was moving too slowly and too noisily. It had to be the wounded doe struggling along. I ran towards the sound. It was not easy country to run through, brushy and full of downed limbs. I made so much noise myself that I could not hear the deer anymore. I had to stop again to listen, and she was still moving but I had gained some ground. I ran a couple of more sprints that way, stopping to listen every thirty yards or so. Then I could make out the deer ahead of me. She was struggling, and it almost looked as though she was rearing up on her hind legs, but the brush kept me from getting a real good view. I ran towards her again and suddenly flew out of the brush and hay, surprised to find myself in the state highway ditch. The doe was struggling, trying to climb up the shoulder of the road, and that is what I had seen through the brush.

Roger was some distance away, so I drew my knife and ran towards the deer and tried to slash its throat. When I got near her she reared up and threw out her front hooves at me. As she did this, she gave a throaty grunt. She lashed at me this way several times, and each time her hooves slashed out at me, she grunted that same way. I reconsidered my approach. I called for Roger. He had heard the deer's grunting, and yelled back, asking me if I was tangling with a bear! I assured him it was the deer, and he hustled over. As he did, I kept moving to get in front of the deer, so she would not move off. She was now having real difficulty moving about. When Roger arrived, we finished her off quickly with another arrow. Then we sat down and laughed at how our chase had concluded. Just minutes after we had her down, the rest of the gang pulled up to help. The deer was dead on the shoulder of the road, so at least we would not have to drag it!

We have had many long and challenging tracking adventures, some ending with frustration. Tim has had a couple of nice bucks get away, including the one mentioned earlier in this book, and another we lost in a driving rain storm. Rain has cost us a few deer. My neighbor, Rex Waters, once hit a buck that presented a very difficult tracking

"It is just a matter of how long it takes, how far they go, and how good you are at staying with them."

The end of a
night-time tracking adventure.

Left to right - Phil Hyry, Jim Schubitzke,
and Tim Tuominen with a daytime recovery.

opportunity. He had hit the buck during his evening hunt. After losing the trail that night, he and I tracked the buck the next morning. It was hit in the gut and liver, but the arrow never made an exit wound, and the gut plugged up the entrance. We had only thirty yards or so of blood trail, yet we were able to follow his tracks in the leaves once we had daylight. We recovered him, 300 yards from where Rex arrowed him. That was a tough one.

My brief hand to hoof combat on the shoulder of the highway with that big doe is not the only such encounter that I am aware of. My cousin, Arlen Hintsala, topped my face-off. While hunting in Black River during the rifle season, he tangled with a buck that Phil had wounded. The buck charged Arlen, and he shot it with a pistol, after fending it off by grabbing the rack. The result was some stitches in the palm for Arlen, and a resting-place in the freezer for the deer.

I think the ideal number for tracking is three people, provided all are either experienced at it, or willing to admit that they are not and follow the instructions of the people who are. One person standing with the last blood, while the other two search, works very well. You can rotate positions as people get sore backs and strained eyes. When you are at a tough check, all three can range out and look for the next drip. I normally do not like four people on the trail. Too many people along the trail just seems to result in the trackers wiping out parts of the trail, especially when they are inexperienced and/or overly anxious trackers. With my regular partners, it is not a problem, because they know their stuff.

There is almost nothing so disappointing as losing the trail of a wounded animal, nor a decision more distasteful than the one to give up on the trail. On the flip side, when you recover an animal under difficult circumstances such as this, it is one of the greatest thrills in hunting. To follow a long, difficult blood trail and come up with the animal, really makes the hunter feel like the complete predator.

Chapter Fourteen
Humble Pie

If you have spent any time at all hunting, you have undoubtedly had occasion to get your butt kicked and your ego deflated by the poor dumb animals you are seeking. You know what I mean—getting whipped. Your pals may not know about it, and everyone you know may think you are the consummate predator who never blows a shot and is always in the right place at the right time. But you and I know differently, don't we? You may have covered it up, but you know I am right. Here is some advice, and take it for what it is worth. I have beat myself up many a time for blowing opportunities, and glossed over or downright fibbed about some of my blunders. Learn to own up to it and to laugh a little at yourself. Be serious about your hunting but not too serious about yourself. You will enjoy yourself a lot more.

I know guys who always have a serious alibi for every miss or miscue they commit. I suspect that these types commit a lot more blunders than they will ever admit to. I have been asked by people with very straight faces, "How did you miss?" and heard them ask other people the same thing. Face it partner, blowing a shot is as easy as falling off a log, and you know darn well it has happened to you. Been there, done that. The longer I hunt, the less I find myself all balled up over a mistake and the less time it takes for me to laugh about it. It has made the whole business much more fun. Try it. I can honestly say that some of my most memorable stories (and I mean fond memories) are those of being humbled. When it's a matter of screwing up, it is funny. When it is a matter of doing things well, but the quarry does everything better, it is downright fascinating. That's what happened to me in the early 80's with my backyard bucks.

We had a lot of deer around my home that year, including a nice pair of small bucks that were regularly feeding in the field, right near the house. There were also many propeller heads around, and my evening watches in the early season were very entertaining in that I got to see many deer. I killed a doe the fourth day of the season, but we had plenty of tags in the group, so I was able to keep hunting. Having secured my winter meat supply, I now wanted one of the bucks. After taking it easy for a couple of days right after getting the doe, I began my campaign against the local antlered ones. It was a circus.

The bucks were showing up at pretty much the same time each evening, and they only stayed in the field by the house for a half-hour or so, then moved on to who knows where. I set up a portable stand on the north side of the field, and the first couple of evenings that I hunted there they showed up, but came out the southwest corner and never quite came into range. I moved the stand to that area and the next time out sat in this new position. My back was to the field, and if they came in on the trails that they had used the previous two visits they would be ten yards or so to my left, which is about as good as it can get for a right handed archer. What actually happened is they came in 10 yards to my right, and I had to worm around in the stand to get into a position to take my shot. These were the days before I was smart enough to use a safety belt, and how I didn't fall right out of the stand with all the twisting and turning I did, I'll never know. The deer bounded off a little ways at the commotion, and I ended up missing about a thirty-yard shot at the larger buck, which I thought to be a 6-pointer.

As it often does, the missed shot wised the deer up to this stand location and on subsequent evenings they varied their entrance point into the field and eluded me. I was growing tired of hunting so close to the house. It was just too much like sitting on the back steps for me, but the bucks were there so what should I do? What I did was move a couple of my hounds out into the field, staking them there on chains and moving their dog houses out to them. I thought the bucks would abandon this field with the dogs there and move to the next closest feeding area, my back field. I could hunt them there. That is precisely what they did, and I managed to miss that same buck there as well. It was a twenty-five yard, broadside shot, and I aimed for just below the chest anticipating that the deer would jump the string. The arrow flew true, but the deer did not jump and the shaft zipped right under him. He jumped back and gave me another shot at about forty yards, and that one went over his back. My brother-in-law, Tim, managed to miss this same buck from the same stand shortly afterwards. This pretty much wised up these two deer to the stand locations and they disappeared for a while.

I continued my hunting, moving to different stand locations as the wind or my mood warranted. We had a stretch of wet weather that raised the Floodwood River (a mile west of my home) above its banks. This flood seemed to move many deer from the river bottom into my home area. The neighbor's field was planted in fresh clover and the deer were going nuts feeding on it. With the influx of flood refugees, there was a band of 15 to 25 deer in this field 24 hours a day. I had not been able to spot anything with antlers. One evening, when I drove by the field on my way home from work, I saw the whole gang was just a short distance from the east side of the field. They were very close to good stalking cover. I saw it as a chance to get close, and if nothing else, get a good look at what was in the group.

I hurriedly got my stuff together and grabbed a handful of something for supper, then headed off to look over the herd. Halfway out to the field, I heard a pitter patter and whine behind me, and there was our little beagle pup running after me. Nuts! I did not want to take the time to bring him back, so I cussed him out a little and tried to chase him back towards home. It looked like it worked as the pup dashed off towards the house, but after walking another hundred yards or so, he showed up again. This time I got a little physical with him and again, he skittered off towards home. I continued my hike, and before long, I had stalked through the wooded pasture to within a hundred yards or so of the deer. I was using small, scattered, balsam trees for cover, and I found a vantagepoint and glassed the field. There were nearly twenty

deer and not an antler to be seen. It was fun to observe though, and
the deer put on a little show for me. It was a cloudy night with very
gusty winds of varying direction. Swirling winds, I guess you would
call them. As usual, the gusting wind made the deer jumpy. Every now
and again, a couple of them would dash off as if they had scented or
spotted trouble. The rest would watch and just stand there. The panicky ones would stop and settle down, then a different group would do
the same thing. About this time, I heard a rustle in the grass, and turning to look behind me, I saw a very sheepish beagle pup sitting in the
grass thirty feet away. He was wagging his tail and telling me with his
expression that he knew I didn't want him along, but if I let him stay,
he would sit there quietly and be good. Okay, good enough.

I turned my attention back to the deer, and as I did, two huge does
and their kids (each had twins), broke off from the herd and came on
the run, in a semi-circular route, over towards me. As they got within
forty yards, they started to separate, mill about, and to feed. Here was
the situation. I was on my knees by a five-foot tall balsam tree. Out in
the field, northwest of me, southwest of me, and at all points between,
were a dozen or more deer, scattered and feeding in the field. South of
me, and about to pass to the east, were six more deer, spread into a line
about thirty yards long. Thirty FEET east of me was a cowering beagle
pup who was getting more and more alarmed because he saw these
half-dozen strange critters moseying in his direction. The wind was
swirling, my hands were getting cold, the puppy was whining, and I
was about to be surrounded by deer. It was a ridiculous picture, and
great fun.

The half-dozen closest animals settled down and fed slowly to the
north until I was, in fact, surrounded. The beagle whimpered and the
deer looked at him and showed no sign of recognition or alarm. One
of the fawns lay down twenty yards from me and chewed its cud. There
was not a stitch of cover betwixt me and several of the deer, and for a
moment, I was tempted to take one of the big does. I pulled on my
gloves and the deer did not notice. The puppy finally panicked, ran
over, and jumped up on me, crying his little heart out. The deer
watched and showed as much interest as they would in a cloud moving by. It was strange. It was as though I was invisible. How none of

the deer winded me with all that swirling air, I will never know. I took a last look around for horns, and when I saw none, I got up and left, finally scaring off the six deer that were all less than thirty yards from me, some only fifteen. As I started towards the house, I scolded the pup once more to get home. This time he went, and did so at a run. He was totally unnerved.

I decided I would sit the rest of the evening in my field that was adjacent to the county road. This was at the opposite the end of the property from where I had just been. Several times, when walking through that field after dark, I had jumped two or three deer. One had always been alone and ran off without blowing or taking the big leaps that does and fawns usually do. Neither did it show its flag as it ran off. These were at least indications of a smart deer, most likely a buck. This deer had always been in the same general area at the same time, so I set up on a tree limb near there and waited. It wasn't long before the familiar pair of bucks, the ones I had been thrashed by earlier in the year, showed up. They crossed the road from the east and into my field. They fed there near the road for a long time, well out of bow range. After a bit, I saw another deer crest the top of the hill to the east. It was heading right towards the other pair at a slow trot. Its head was low and with its neck stretched out, and his whole posture and movement told me it was a mature buck, even before I saw the rack. As it got to the road, I did see the rack, and it was a decent one.

The big guy crossed the road and joined the other two, but not for a friendly chat. He rushed, head down, at first one and then the other, chasing them off in opposite directions. They never even thought about standing up to him, but bounded off until he quit pursuing, then watched him with very nervous suspicion. The boss resumed his purposeful gait on the same original heading, which was right towards me. I readied the bow and tried to calm myself down. It looked as though I was going to get a crack at a decent buck.

When he was fifty yards away, I suddenly heard activity at the neighbor's house just north of us. The buck slowed, then stopped and looked in that direction. I heard the neighbor start his Cadillac. I should say, the Cadillac that had no muffler. The show was over. Mr. Buck turned and dashed off to where he had come from, leaving me to cuss my luck and my neighbor.

It was pretty clear to me now what was happening here. This buck was traveling from his bedding area east of my place, crossing my land, and checking on that big herd of deer to the west, hoping to find a doe in season. I had been encountering him after dark on occasion when walking out from my evening hunts in the back field. It appeared that after entering my east field, he would look the area over and feed for a while. Then, he would turn to his left onto a tractor road, and follow this road along my south fence line. He would follow this to the back field and beyond, to where the local herd was gathered. It was a good situation for me. I lived between this buck that I wanted, and some very effective bait. I now knew the route he was taking. This is how the chess game began, and it went on for two weeks or so.

I hunted this same small area of his route every evening. He did not always show before dark, and if it was starting to get dark and he was not in sight, I would leave, to avoid spooking him on my way out. The next time I saw him, he got within bow range. It wasn't an open shot, and he sensed something out of place, leaving before giving me a shot. I moved the stand slightly and into better cover. It had an even more limited area to shoot through, but that area was right on his trail at ten yards or so, and the heavier cover would conceal me nicely. The next sighting brought him to about twenty-five yards, coming right to that trail, but again he sensed danger and stopped. He stood for a long time, looking down the trail in front of him. He was sniffing the air, not looking nervous, but like the wary critter he was. He was aware of danger nearby, but not in a panic. He just coolly assessed the situation and considered his options. For the most part, cover obscured him, but I watched his face through the intervening branches. I saw when he blinked and when his nose wiggled as it tested the air. His head would turn every little while, just slightly. First right, then left, and back again.

If you don't hunt, or you haven't been in spitting distance of a nice buck but unable to shoot, you have no idea of the tension level that exists in that circumstance. I had invested many hours into getting a shot at this guy. Here he was, so close I could almost taste him, but with the cover and the weapon I was using, he may as well have been on the moon. Everything hung on that moment and what he would do. Once he decided, he would be in my sights in five seconds, or gone in less time than that. He never actually looked towards me, but suddenly he turned and trotted back to the east, leaving me defeated, deflated, and hanging on to my stand like a used water balloon. Man, what a rush!

After this encounter, he changed his routine by leaping the south fence, a hundred yards from my stand site, and following it west, passing out of bow range from the stand locations. I made a new plan to lay on my belly in some long grass by the fence. The buck was jumping the fence near a couple of trees that were not big enough or thick enough to use for stand sites. However, they would provide a small blind spot that would allow me to get to my knees and draw when he jumped the wire. The game continued.

I also hunted him in the mornings. I only saw him once early in the day. I had just left my stand site far to the east of my place, and had moved back into my field where I had been hunting this character. As I neared my evening stand location on the edge of the trees, I jumped deer just inside the woods. I moved around in a wide circle to try to cut them off. I succeeded, but again spooked them without getting a look. I retraced my circling route, but before I regained my old position, the place where I had been when I originally jumped this group, they came busting out of the woods and across my field. What a picture it was! It was a sunny, frosty morning. The buck was actually herding two does back toward his bedding area. He moved like one of those cow ponies. Each time a doe changed direction, he would dash out to the side of her and push her back onto the eastward course. I have never seen anything like it since. I had been outfoxed, again.

The last move of the chess game came on a Sunday night just before rifle season. Sherilee was off somewhere and I was watching the boys, who were pretty little at the time. Sherilee had promised to be home at a certain time that would allow me to get into my "prone" stand position in time to intercept my adversary. She was late. I rushed out to the fence line, cutting through the woods to keep in cover. I was worried that he might be in the field already and that he would see me. As it turned out, I was just a hair late. Before I reached my planned ambush site, he jumped the fence. I was stalking down the fence line all stooped over, huffing and puffing from my double quick trip. He moved out into the field and galloped past me, spotting me when I drew the bow and kind of laughing at me when I zinged a desperation shot under his belly at about 35 yards. He was gone in a few seconds, and he quit using the route through my field after that. I saw him one more time, and that was when he was hanging dead in my neighbor's barn. He got him during the rifle season.

The fun I had during this two-week contest was about as exciting as any hunting I have done. I guess the only time it is better is when you manage to come out on top. I never used to admit to taking that desperation shot, because it was a lousy shot to take. It was too long a shot for my skills and the deer was running. A person should not take poor shots. That is what I did, and I am sorry I fibbed about it before. Now that I own up to it, I am healed.

I did get another doe that year, but the deer with horns gave me a whipping. Three different bucks dodged my arrows, and several others showed themselves and got away without me getting a shot. They kicked my butt.

I have taken many other beatings from game. Some were long, involved affairs like the one just related. Others were quick, ugly beatings, dished out by a variety of critters, some with brains smaller than a pea. I once knelt in my canoe and carefully paddled up to a flock of twelve mallard drakes, trying to look like a drifting log. I moved the paddle in slow motion and kept it low over the boat when I brought it over to switch the side I was paddling on, which you must do to keep a canoe going straight. It was a difficult, but well executed stalk. When I got to within thirty yards, I straightened up, shouldered the gun, and laughed aloud when I looked down the barrel. There I saw a huge clump of weeds slung over it, totally obscuring the end of the barrel. The birds flushed and I let them go without shooting. Obviously, when I had passed the paddle over the boat, I had dragged the weeds across and many fell off the paddle and onto my shotgun. When the birds flushed, I could not even see the end of the gun. I chuckled all the way back to the truck.

My dad used to laugh about an incident where he was humiliated by a pair of deer while hunting in Black River, in the good old days. It happened during his prime, and he claimed that in his prime any running deer he shot at—within a hundred yards—was a goner. Considering he never was one to brag, I take this as fact. On the day in question, he was on stand on a railroad grade while a drive was being made. This drive was one of their regular operations, and the fleeing deer always followed a certain routine when crossing the grade. There were high banks on each side of the grade, and the deer would jump from one bank onto the grade, then with one more leap reach the far bank. There was still open shooting for the stander on that far side as well. This particular morning was frosty, and there was no snow. The leaves and litter on the ground were very noisy. Dad heard a pair of deer crunching the leaves and crashing the brush as they approached the grade in their flight from the drivers. They would pass in very good range from him, and he prepared himself. He was thinking that if one of these deer were a buck, it would cross the grade after the doe. He would let the doe go, and take the buck when it landed on the grade.

Just as he had it pictured in his mind, the doe landed on the grade, then leaped to the far side, and was on her way. The second deer was a few seconds behind, and Dad was primed and ready. He saw the deer, and it was a nice buck. Then to his surprise, the buck leaped the entire grade in one jump, landing on the far bank! As Dad told the story, he still had plenty of open ground to get a good shot, but the surprise move by the buck completely blew his cool and he fired several shots, none of which came even close. That's hunting for you.

Chapter Fifteen
Almost Perfect

In the last chapter, I fessed up to some of my blunders. Now I am going to brag, for like all dedicated hunters who have practiced their craft for a length of time, there have been moments when my performance has been perfection itself. Okay, maybe not perfection, but there have been times when I did darn good. If it has happened to you, and I am sure it has, then you know how terrific it feels.

My earlier story about the turkey I killed was an example of a day I consider my performance to be top shelf. It is not that I did everything right, but it was an encounter that lasted a long time. I was locked up with that bird the entire morning. There were plenty of chances to mess it up, but even if I made a miscue or two, I was able to recover from them and the story ended as a great success for me.

A few other examples come to mind. I had a grouse hunt over my dog not many years ago when I killed my limit of five birds in less than ninety minutes. I never got to work three-fourths of the coverts I had planned to hunt that evening. I once killed eleven ducks with fourteen shots, which is as good as I will ever do on ducks. The limit that year was three birds per day, so this good shooting covered at least four days. What was also significant about that streak, was that these ducks came down graveyard dead, and there was no time spent chasing down or losing cripples.

When I killed my second bear, I began the best shooting streak I have ever had with my bow. Over a three or four year span, with five shots, I killed four bucks and the bear. For a guy who had missed a bear three times at eight yards in one evening, this was quite an improvement! I told my pals that if I got one more, I was going to rename my bow from Maggie, to Maggie Sixkiller. That was enough to jinx me, and the next season I blew an easy 25-yard shot at a buck feeding under my stand. You would think a person would learn to keep their mouth shut. However, this chapter is my good stuff, okay? Another day, when I managed to do most everything right, ended with a wall-hanger deer.

In 1982, I was bow hunting just across the road from my home. The fields there had been planted in corn. I had never hunted in corn before because our area is poor country for growing it, and few people bothered trying. Our local deer had probably never had the opportunity to sample this kind of food, so it did not pull in as many animals as one might think. The deer I had seen feeding there seemed to be more interested in the weeds growing in among the corn stalks. I have read that deer instinctively feed on the highest protein foods available at any one time. I noticed myself, that in the fall, when we turned over the soil in our vegetable garden and flowerbeds, the deer really took after the weeds that sprouted up. I am told that new growth on plants contain much protein.

I had seen a smaller buck in this field a couple of times, but never close enough to shoot. One evening, I was on my way to hunt the field and was stalking the area where this buck usually fed, just in case he was already in the field. I didn't think it very likely, because the sun was still high above the horizon and the deer usually didn't hit the fields until after it had gone down. As I walked, hunched over and moving along a gully near where the buck often fed, I heard a sudden rattle in the corn to my left. When I looked up, there was a beauty of a buck, streaking out of the field. He held his head high and the sun caught the rack and the golden brown and white of his hide. I was left standing in the open field with my mouth agape. Seeing a buck of this size in the field at that time of day was very unusual. The bad part of it was that the mature bucks usually got nocturnal after you jumped them out of a field. I thought my first look at him might also be my last. The field was a good spot to hunt even if this larger buck did not come back, so I kept hunting there, and tried to set up to intercept him should he ever come back.

Sherilee saw the buck on the road a couple of times, after dark. I saw his tracks several times. He was often travelling with a smaller deer that turned out to be a fork buck, a different deer from the one I had seen in the cornfield earlier. I selected a stand site on a fence line that divided two fields, both of which had corn in them. The portable stand was set up in a balsam on the east/west running fence line. I would sit facing east, which was the direction from which the buck usually came into the corn. On my left, the field was a hundred yards wide, and it ran behind me almost a quarter-mile to the county road. If I looked to my right, I was looking straight down the east edge of the second field, where it met the trees and brush. I hunted this stand whenever the wind was right and saw two different bucks and several does. The does gave what would have been good shots, but I passed on them. The big buck had not shown himself again in daylight.

It was a late October evening with plenty of wind when I again took the stand. I had really been enjoying my time in this stand because the corn pulled in a lot of non-game wildlife that I watched with great interest. On this particular night, I heard movement to my right as the sun went down. A buck, not the big one, was moving into the field. As I spotted him, he appeared to look right at me, and I froze. He was twenty yards away and in the brush, so I could not be positive he was looking at me. In that situation, you have to assume that they are, and I had to be still and wait him out. This turned out to take longer than I would have imagined, and I could hear additional rustling in the corn on my left. Finally, the buck looked away and I was able to turn and look to my left. There, at the east end of the field, was my big buck. Ahead of him and leading the way into the field was a nice fork buck, the regular companion of the bigger deer. Straight to the north of me were two nice does that I had seen often, and had declined to shoot at on a couple of evenings. I was now surrounded.

The deer began to feed among the broken down stalks of corn. The two does, along with the fork-horn, soon fed towards my stand. Shortly, they were within bow range. The larger one stayed in the middle of the field, now straight north of me. This was a high stress situation. There were five deer around me now, and three of them were bucks. The first one I had seen was now somewhere behind me, but I couldn't be sure where. If I raised the bow to shoot he might well be looking right at me at the time, and I would be cooked. If I turned to look for him, I would have my eyes off the other four deer. Then, to turn back towards them, the risk would be four times as great of having one of the four looking at me. I ignored the one behind me and concentrated on the small herd that was now within fifty yards.

The does and fork buck presented any number of chances to shoot, but I just was not going to do that with the big buck there. It seemed to take forever for him to start heading towards me, but at last, he did. From about thirty yards out, he came walking right in, but he was coming straight on so I could not get a good shot. When he finally turned and I began to draw, he stepped right behind the smaller buck! I was at full draw and waited as long as I could, but had to let off when the deer continued to stand, screened behind the smaller deer. Then, something alerted the deer and they all snapped their heads up and looked off behind me. I thought it was all over. However, whatever had alerted the deer turned out to be something they could tolerate, for they went back to feeding. The big buck then walked straight away, so again I had no good shot. He stopped to feed at about thirty-five yards out. This had gone on for about forty minutes or so. This kind of situation is fun. I get so full of adrenaline that when the situation goes on and on as this one was doing, it is actually exhausting. That evening, as I watched this herd, I went from the rush, to the shaking, to the exhaustion. Finally, I reached a state that, while not calm, was at least rather controlled. I usually find myself fighting back a smile, and on this night, just as I have in other similar situations, I told myself that no matter what happened with the situation that I had on my hands, this was fun! The fact that these deer can do this to you!

It was now beginning to get dark, and I knew that I had to do something soon. The buck was farther out than I am comfortable with, but the wind had died and I could take a relaxed shot. Okay, relaxed is not the best term, but relatively speaking, I would be able to take my time with this shot. Right up until the last, I considered shooting the fork horn, which was only ten yards away. No guts, no glory. I shot at the big one.

The arrow flashed outward in its long ballistic arc and smacked into the buck just above the centerline of his body, and in the rear lung area. He had not jumped the string, but at the shot had raised his head. When the arrow struck, he was off like a rocket. I got out of the stand and had to shoo away a couple of the other deer when I hit the ground. I walked over to the spot where my target had been standing and left my safety belt there as a marker. I headed for home to call for help, trying to replay in my mind what I saw after the arrow hit. Where was the arrow? What angle was the deer at when it hit? How did he run? All of these are important pieces of information that can help you in recovering the deer. My neighbors, Jim Liubakka and Rex Waters, came out to assist me in the tracking. From the start, it looked good. The only bad omen was when we heard coyotes yipping in the area where the buck had been headed. I yelled at the top of my lungs to scare them off, lest they beat us to my buck. Of course, it was dark now, and we trailed with the aid of flashlights.

The buck had left the field and crossed the powerline. On the powerline right-of-way, we found good blood sign. When we got into the woods on the far side of the line, in a small clone of four to six-inch diameter popple, we were stunned at what we saw. The buck must have been trying to wipe off the arrow in his side. There were huge smears of blood on the trees, some of them 18 inches wide. We found the back end of the arrow there. At that point, we were confident we would find him soon. I had seen where I hit him and thought I had hit one lung and the liver. Our confidence dropped a short while later when the blood trail started to peter out. Soon we were casting, as a trailing beagle does, around the last spot of blood. We found occasional smears or drops, but it was very hard work to do so. At one point, he traveled through long swamp hay. It looked like the only blood being left behind was that which was wiped off the protruding end of the shaft, by the long, stiff, spikes of grass. One of the lights began to go dead.

We went for long stretches of time without seeing blood. We would have one person stand at the last spot of blood with the burnt out light; the other two would cast ahead for more sign. We kept the

"I had every opportunity to blow the chance... for once, I did not!"

The author with his best archery trophy, a 13-point whitetail.

trail by using this maneuver a couple of times. Finally, we had a very long check while I was marking the last blood. Jim and Rex circled and circled, finally calling out that they had found a little spot of blood. I had the nearly dead flashlight off, but we were in the hay swamp. I could clearly see my partners, looking over this latest spoor, about fifty yards off. I began walking towards them through the long grass, and when halfway there, I stepped on something that felt a little unusual. It felt like a deer leg. I snapped on the dim light, and sure enough, there he was. When I called to my friends that I had just stepped on the deer, they did not believe me. They were not convinced until I started counting his points aloud. He was a nice, mature buck with 13 points on his rack. He ended up weighing out at 171 pounds.

It was around eleven when we got him back to the house, where Sherilee and Jim's wife, Karen, were visiting while their foolish men stumbled around the swamps in black night looking for a deer. They were impressed with the buck, and so was I. He was the best trophy I have ever taken with bow, and he is mounted on my den wall. I often look at that mount and reminisce about that night and all the effort that went into the hunt, and the high drama that resulted. It began when I first saw the buck, fleeing the field with bright sunshine on his antlers. When I finally had the encounter that gave me a shot, it was a long and drawn out affair. I have killed deer that just walked out and took a bullet or an arrow, the whole thing being over in ten seconds. The encounter with this buck had me surrounded by a small group of deer. Five noses, five pairs of eyes and ears. To be that close, to that many, for that long… well, it is exhausting, exciting, and very hard to do. I had every opportunity to blow the chance, and finally, for once, I did not! It ended in storybook fashion, finding the deer in the dark of night, with twinkling stars over our heads and the music of owls and coyotes in our ears. It was almost perfect.

Chapter Sixteen
Old Mossy Horns

A mong all the deer taken by my hunting cronies, friends, family, or even acquaintances, one is clearly the best trophy. It is the one taken by my brother-in-law, Jeweleon Tuominen, in 1968. Jeweleon was in his late teens when he killed this monster. It dressed out at nearly 300 pounds. The rack is a massive, non-typical, with approximately twenty distinctive points. The main beams are massive and a bit misshapen, the brow tines are beautiful, long, and each has a sweeping curve. This incredible trophy was taken on the last day of the rifle season when it wandered into a hayfield in broad daylight. Jeweleon's mother, who was doing dishes at the kitchen sink, spotted it through the kitchen window and mistook it for a moose. The hunters were all relaxing in the house at the time. After a mad scramble for a gun, the deer had crossed the road and gone out of sight. Jeweleon was able to pick it out again, across a swamp, and made a successful shot at over 200 yards.

To say that luck played a big role in Jeweleon getting the deer of a lifetime would be an understatement. However, there are not many lads in their teens that could make the shot that he did. There is some measure of luck in every successful hunt. When there is a disproportionate amount of it, there is no shame. You have had, or will have, plenty of occasions to miss an opportunity through getting no luck, or the wrong kind of it. Personally, I am pleased that a man who has an appreciation for the quality of the trophy took this buck. In addition, he became an accomplished hunter. He studies his quarry and approaches hunting with hard work and intensity. He is one of the best marksmen I know. If he did not exactly put in his dues before he killed his monster buck, he has more than done so since. Far better when a real hunter takes such an animal, than when some casual nimrod lucks into one.

We all know someone who has taken an exceptional buck under similar circumstances. Killing a deer, like Jeweleon's 1968 monster, is something we deer hunters yearn for. There is another trophy, however, that a hunter yearns for even more. This is the trophy buck that is known before he falls. The local buck that all the neighbors know about and that has escaped encounters with hunters, often several times. If you have been hunting deer or been around deer hunters for very long, you have heard about Old Mossy Horns. Maybe not by that name, because I have heard him called Old Julius, Splayed, Homer, The Elk, and a dozen other names. Of course, I am talking about "the big one" that roams a fellow's hunting area. For myself, and I am sure many others, the very best thing that could happen to us in our hunting career would be to bag one of these legendary bucks that everyone in the neighborhood has heard about. Old Mossy does not come along very often. In twenty years plus of deer hunting in Cedar Valley, only twice have I been conscious of his presence.

Homer was the big buck that frequented our woods for three seasons or so. I saw his tracks several times, and they were distinctive. We laid eyes on him twice, and several of the neighbors saw him as well. He used our woods mostly as a travel-way, cruising through during the rut and pre-rut times, looking for new romantic conquests. One year, during the night before the opening day of rifle season, he was all over the property, tearing up trees and making huge scrapes everywhere. He even thumbed his nose at us by walking around the yard and circling the dog kennel a couple of times. We saw the tracks in our flashlights when we left for our stands in the morning. What he was doing around the kennel, I cannot tell you. One of the bitches was in heat and maybe the estrogen scent attracted him. Maybe he was just looking for a fight.

Both times we saw him were during the season, in broad daylight, and we were armed. Yours truly played a major role in him getting away without anyone firing a shot.

The first time was opening day the year we got 36 inches of snow a few days before the season. Getting around was very tough, and although the deer usually leave our woods as soon as the snow gets deep, all of our plans had been to hunt there on opening day. The storm gave us no time to adequately plan or scout another area. We decided to take our chances and hunt the stands behind the house as originally intended. It was Ben, Danny, and I. Danny took a stand on the south end of "the big pond" in the hopes that the neighbors annual opening day drive would push some deer towards him. I had intended to tell him not to sit in the seat that was in the stand, but rather stand up and face the seat. This would have put him looking into an open ash swamp where I thought the deer might pass through. It would also put the main trail to his left; perfect for a right-handed shooter as he is. Right after we split up, I realized that I had neglected to give him these instructions. When he got into the stand, he naturally sat down on the seat to be more comfortable during his vigil.

The neighbors got their drive going earlier than usual. Before it was underway long, Danny heard something on the trail to his right and just slightly behind him. He looked carefully over his shoulder, and there was Homer, run out of the neighbors place and walking down the trail, only twenty-five yards from my boy. Had I given Danny the intended instructions, and had he followed them, he would almost certainly have seen the buck coming from eighty yards off and been able to mount the gun easily to prepare for the shot. As it was, he was hand-cuffed, and the buck stopped to check out the situation. Danny was debating what to do when the buck turned around and dashed back the way he had come.

Later, when we got together and heard Danny's story, the boys took stands on likely crossings, as I took Homer's trail. The buck had a nice rack, but the body size was more impressive. Looking at his hoofprints made you tingle. I followed the tracks only a hundred yards from where he and Danny had met, and jumped him from his bed. I never saw him or heard him go, but the sign told the tale. He had heard me coming,

got up from the bed, and walked to a small, thick stand of young balsam. There, he used the trees for cover and stood watching his back
trail, I suppose until he saw me. Then he left on the run. He really felt
pressure now with someone on his tracks, because he headed east and
crossed 250 yards of open field. I heard a barrage from the powerline a
quarter-mile off and figured it was directed at this buck. Later, my
neighbors confirmed they had taken shots at him, but missed.

The next season, we were again hunting in our woods on opening
weekend. Three of us took stands for evening watch one afternoon,
everyone sitting in stands that I had picked for them. My wife's cousin,
Doug Miller, was hunting with us. He had suggested putting someone
in the back field. I said it was probably the fourth-best spot, and if we
had four people one would go there, but under the present circumstances we should leave that area open. That is what we did. Naturally,
just a short while after I took my stand, I looked towards the back field
just in time to see Homer gallop across it. He was over two hundred
yards away, and I only saw him for a second, but the rack was a nice
heavy one. The next day I checked the tracks, and he had come into
the field at a lope, right between two stands. A man in either stand
would have had shooting, the one stand within forty or fifty yards. As
the deer reached the south end of the field he slowed to a walk, and
went within five feet of another of my stands.

I saw Homer's tracks for one or two more seasons, but never got
another look at him. He isn't around any more, at least in my bailiwick.
I never heard of anyone bagging him. Maybe he is still out there, bigger and smarter than ever.

The Elk first appeared in about 1988. The Elk never crossed my
path, so I don't know for sure, but it sounded like he would make
Homer look small. Several people saw him over several years, many of
them being relatives or hunting pals of mine. Cousin Rod, and broth-
er-in law, Roger, each got a look at him while bow hunting, Rod missing a shot. During one rifle season, he showed up at Aunt Eva's place
as the folks there were leaving for church. Broad daylight and open season, and he stood in the field right by the county road. Eva's son-in-
law, Ron, at first mistook him for a piece of farm equipment! I believe
the Elk met his doom in 1992. My wife's cousin, Bill, was crossing the

fields by Eva's place in the early morning, about to make a drive to three other members of his group. In a little secluded field, rather hidden from the road and farmhouses, the big buck jumped at Bill's approach and loped towards the woods. However, he stopped to look back. It was a shot of over a hundred yards, but Bill (shooting off hand) drilled the bruiser through the neck and dropped him right there. He was a beau-

"Most of us will never see, much less get a chance, at Old Mossy Horns. However, each time we take the field to hunt deer, there is that small chance that he will be ours."

Jeweleon Tuominen with his outstanding buck, 1968.

tiful 11-pointer with long heavy beams. I was surprised to find he weighed only around 200 even, because I saw him hanging and would have guessed 225 at least. Two hundred pounds though, is still a heck of a whitetail. I don't know for sure if Bill's deer is the Elk or not. It is a terrific trophy. However, I hope the Elk is out there waiting for me!

Another huge whitetail roamed my dad's hunting turf in the fifties. Several people saw him over a period of several years. Cousin Chas actually got a crack at him once or twice. The last time he was seen was when Dad's gang was making a drive to a railroad grade, and the big guy zipped across the tracks at very long range from my dad. As the deer ran up a long, wooded hill a couple hundred yards off, Dad took several shots with the old 300 Savage. They found hair and a little blood, but a lack of snow caused their tracking efforts to fail. The buck was never seen again.

Most of us will never see, much less get a chance, at Old Mossy Horns. However, each time we take the field to hunt deer, there is that small chance that he will be ours. Perhaps that is one reason we do not hang up our gun.

Chapter Seventeen
Overnighter on the West Branch

A s the duck season progresses each year, the birds that still linger on my favorite river seem to congregate further and further downstream. This makes sense, for ducks react to hunting pressure and the most hunting pressure occurs where the hunters can gain access most easily. The days have grown shorter and shorter. It is more difficult to cover the far corners of my hunting grounds in a day of paddling, unless I skip the usual morning decoy hunting and begin paddling and jump shooting at the first break of day.

There is a place on the river where an old, manmade, drainage ditch intersects the river, far downstream from any easy access. It is the spot most likely to hold birds at any given time of day throughout the season. To hunt here in the first light of morning, I have to leave the house at least two hours before legal shooting time, and will have ninety minutes of paddling to do during that time. I've done this on many occasions, and also hunted in the evening and spent two hours after dark getting myself home. The situation begs for an overnight trip. A few years back, near the end of my duck season, I decided to head down and spend the night.

My pals, Rex and Bernie, were planning to hunt the river with me in the morning. I left word with their wives that I was going in that afternoon and spending the night. They were planning to shoot over decoys that evening and then paddle downriver in the morning. I would hook up with them when they came down.

I went in about noon, starting from the bridge where I often access the river. This point is about a two and one-half hour paddle from the spot where I intended to camp, but this paddling time can result in productive jump shooting if the birds are there. Late in the season, the bigger flocks of mallards might drop in to any spot on the river to spend a few hours, or a few days. The same with Canada geese. I had a couple of different places in mind that might be suitable for camping. They were very close to the area I wanted to set up decoys for the evening and morning shoots I was planning. I would take no tent, just a tarp and sleeping bag, a bit of food, and the hunting gear. Of course my dog, Jill, would be with me as well.

I paddled for over an hour without seeing a single bird. I was still on the stretch of river that sees the most pressure. However, I had expected to see a few birds here. Then, in the distance, I saw a lone bird coming towards me. I got the gun up, ready, and saw that it was a male hooded merganser. It looked to be nicely colored out. It would be a long shot, but here was a chance at a bird I might like to have mounted. When he passed at the closest point of his path to my location, I took a shot. It was a clean miss, but at the report, about 60 geese got up from a side pool only a hundred yards below me. Had I not taken this marginal shot, I may well have paddled right up to this flock. I watched them form up and head for the horizon. Jill and I looked at each other, and I shrugged off her disapproval.

I paddled on and went past the pool where the flock had been. We call this, and a similar pool just below it, the "teal pools," for they often hold some greenwing teal throughout the season. At the second teal pool I jumped three more geese. They got up on my left, and headed upstream parallel to the channel where I was floating. I got up the gun and dumped one of them with my second shot. The momentum from my paddling, along with the current, had me moving along downstream as I shot. I had a window of visibility into the pool through the channel that connects it to the river. When the goose hit the water, it righted itself immediately. It was about 35 yards from me at that moment and I quickly fired my third round at the head and neck in hopes that I could kill it or disable it further. It showed no reaction to the shot, and I reached for my second shotgun, which was loaded and ready in the canoe. My window was quickly closing as the canoe drifted downstream, and I took two quick shots at the goose, the second just as the grass and cattails intervened and blocked my vision.

I sent Jill on the retrieve as I traded the gun for the paddle. With no small amount of effort, I got the boat stopped and turned back upstream. I paddled back to the channel and saw that the goose was dead. I paddled over and picked it up and hoisted Jill into the boat by the collar, a move we have perfected with years of practice. It was a lesser Canada goose, the middle-sized variety. We had our first bird of the trip.

I saw a couple of other birds on the way to my campsite, but none got up in range. When I finally got to the first place I thought might provide a decent camping spot, I was disappointed. The little island in the marsh was covered with chewed off stubs of brush—willow and alder—where the beaver had taken the small trees down. These were sharp, as beaver chewed stumps are, and I could not find an area big enough to lie down that was free of these little spears. The only place that was free of the little harpoons was on the narrow pathways, made by the beaver as they dragged their food supply to the huge feed pile, in the river, next to their lodge. There, I threw down the tarp and my sleeping bag on top of it. I took the other camping gear out of the canoe and arranged it around my bed. Now it was time to hunt.

I paddled down to that little honey hole that always seems to have birds and jumped eight or so mallards from the rushes, killing a nice drake. I set up my decoys and pushed the canoe into the willows to wait for sundown and, hopefully, some ducks. I had only been waiting for perhaps fifteen minutes when a flock of about ten mallards came along. They passed me by and seemed intent on landing at a particular bend upstream where I had first considered setting up. I worked the call and got them to think twice. The bulk of the flock really wanted that spot upstream, but it seemed as though I had convinced a couple of them that my location was better. One pair broke away and came down to look my spread over. It was plain that I had caused some dissension in the ranks, for the pair, and the rest of the group, seemed to be arguing over where to land. Apparently, duckdom is a democracy, for the majority finally started to pitch in upstream and my wayward pair broke off their approach and headed upstream as well. I had one chance at them and dropped the drake with a shot that pleased me. Jill made the retrieve and I had two nice greenheads to go with my honker.

Now I was in a bit of a situation. Any birds that came along would have to choose between me and my plastic flock, being helped—or hurt—by my amateurish calling, and a real flock of birds that really quacked and were swimming around. I wondered if I should paddle upstream to jump them out, and maybe get a shot in the process. After the long paddle down and setting up the camp and the decoys, my tired body urged me to consider my options carefully and to take my time doing so. He who hesitates can be lost, but in this case he would be more rested.

I was still considering my options when I turned to look downstream. I probably gasped aloud at what I saw. A flock of about 40 mallards, in V formation, was gliding right over me on set wings. I could have shot, but they were high. I decided that, competition or not, I would try to call them back. I got them circling, but they were a bit far, and they wanted to set down with their cousins upstream. I got a few circles, but at long range, and they finally pitched in with the others upstream. There was not much legal shooting time left, so I pushed the canoe out of my hiding spot and paddled up to them.

When I jumped them, I hit one that glided a couple of hundred yards into the weeds, and I dropped another nearby. The cripple that had glided off would be a hopeless retrieve for Jill, considering the flooded grass she would need to get through with little or no assistance from me. It was a lost bird, so I called her in to fetch the closer bird, and pushed my canoe into the weeds so I could stand and look for the bird and help my dog. While we were looking for this bird, the sun started to set, and suddenly small groups of mallards were pitching in around us. I was so intent on finding the downed bird that I missed several shooting chances, just because I did not see the birds until they flared and zoomed out of range. Finally, I picked up the gun, watched the sky, and knocked down another drake from a flock of five that came in close. I stopped shooting at mallards then, as I had two greenheads in the boat and two more in the weeds where Jill was searching. We found one but lost the other. Evidently it was still alive and outswam Jill in the thick grass.

There were only minutes left of legal shooting now, and I heard geese. Three of them came over me, quite high, but my second shot folded one. It splashed down, thirty yards into the weeds on the far side of the river. I paddled to that far bank and sent in Jill. She had seen that bird come down and really wanted it. She had just lost a bird. Often, it seems when that happens, she is exceptionally anxious to make amends on her next opportunity. She tore into the flooded grass and would jump to a hummock and stand on her hind legs, looking for the bird, putting her nose in the air to test the wind. She found it quickly and brought it to the boat. It was another lesser Canada. I headed down to pick up the decoys, then paddled back to camp, only a couple hundred yards away.

I cooked a can of soup and dished up some canned food for my partner. It was turning cold and the sky was crystal-clear. There was no moon that night. It was a beautiful fall evening and I had a nice stringer of ducks and geese. At dusk, the air had been filled with chuckling mallards and honking geese, and most of the ducks had set down just below camp, right where we intended to hunt in the morning. Things were looking good. By the time I crawled into the sleeping bag there was frost on everything.

My tarp and bag were set down on that beaver trail, as it was the only place I could find free of the sharp stumps left by the beaver's cutting. During the first hours of darkness, the beavers were slapping their tails in alarm at the apparition blocking their roadway. The lodge was only 50 feet from my bed. Jill snuggled up to me, and every once in a while growled when a beaver got too close. It was getting chilly and I brought her in the bag with me.

It was so pretty out there that night. There was no wind and no moon. The stars shine so brightly when you are away from any man-made light. The air was crisp and clean and the cold bit my cheeks a little, but my stocking cap kept my head warm. My dog and the sleeping bag did the same for the rest of me. It was not the most comfortable of beds, but I was one tired cowboy, and soon I was dreaming.

Strange beds make for restless nights for me under the best of conditions, and these were far from being the best. I began to toss and turn, trying to get comfortable. In doing so, I managed to break the zipper on the sleeping bag. The cold reached in quickly, so I had to get up and do a repair. It was 3:00 A.M. when I began fiddling with it, holding my little flashlight in my mouth for illumination. I managed to make the repair, got zipped up, and warm again. The frost was heavier now, and again I enjoyed the beauty of the night until I drifted off to the sound of the barred owls and the occasional slap of a beaver tail on the water.

It seemed like only minutes had gone by when my little, battery-operated alarm clock, beeped at me. I clicked on the light and looked at the thick frost that coated everything except the sleeping bag, which was damp from my body heat leaking through. It took no small measure of resolve to leave that warm sleeping bag and slide into my cold waders. I cooked some coffee and heated water for instant oatmeal on my little backpack stove. After this quick breakfast, we paddled down to the place where I had been set up the previous evening.

A half-dozen ducks flew out as I paddled down the river, but after that, nothing flew. I could not believe it. During the night, the ducks had disappeared. We watched empty skies. Later in the morning, when Bernie and his brother-in-law, Mike, came through, they moved no birds to us. We chatted for a while from our canoes and then they continued on, planning to paddle through to Bernie's home several miles downstream. I gathered up my decoys and broke camp. I loaded the gear into the canoe and secured my two geese and three greenheads to the top of my waterproof camp box with a bungy cord.

It would be my last duck hunt of the Minnesota season, and although the last day was a bust, the trip was unforgettable. I took my sweet time paddling back upstream. The sun was shining and the frost had burned away. I knew as I paddled along that quiet river, that I would remember this outing for a long time. I killed some birds, but that was nothing unusual. The cold, frosty night though, and sleeping under those star-filled skies, now that was something a person does not see or experience every day. I smiled to myself a lot on my return trip, and I talked aloud to my dog. I could not have asked for a better close to another duck season.

*"I set up my decoys and pushed the canoe into the willows to wait for
sundown and, hopefully, some ducks."*

Jill, the author's constant companion in the duck marsh.

Chapter Eighteen
My Gosh, I'm the Old Timer

Most of us do not really appreciate the pain our parents went through raising us until we raise our own kids. This applies to taking your kids hunting and fishing, just as it does to the real important lessons in life. When you are rather intense in your pursuit of trout or ducks or deer, it can be a bit stressful to have a young protege along. It can also be very entertaining.

During the period when most of the events in this book occurred, I was also raising a family. I have two sons, Ben and Danny, and my youngest child is a girl, named Tara. They all got plenty of lessons in hunting, fishing, and nature. It was fun to be the teacher. Besides my own kids, there have been nieces and nephews, my kid's pals, and the children of my hunting buddies. My own kids had my hunting buddies and their uncles as teachers in the woods as well. This is a worthy pursuit for the old-timer. It can introduce the youngster to things that will enrich their life. It helps to keep this wonderful tradition going, and it is an insurance policy. One day, one of the kids you helped out might get you out to the duck blind or deer stand on a day when you wouldn't have been able to go. Life flies by. As I write this I say, "My gosh! I'm the old-timer!"

With my own kids, it started with walks in the woods. I pointed out the birds and animals or the signs they left behind. If I came home with game I showed it to the kids and answered their questions. I described my experiences outdoors and tried to convey to them how much I enjoyed those experiences. They all took interest, at least for a while. They all learned some things that they will probably keep with them for the rest of their lives. I think at times I tried too hard or was too intense. I am a little outdoorsier than most people, especially in the non-hunting areas. My son, Danny, and his pals, called me Marty Stouffer, after the wildlife filmmaker. It seemed to them I lived in the woods, and when I could not carry a gun, I had the camcorder. Once, I asked a young fellow who planned to hunt with us, about his experience with guns. He told me he had had firearm safety training. Danny was there, and he announced, "You haven't had my Dad's firearms safety training yet!" I took that as a compliment.

I spoke a lot about guns to the kids. I learned to shoot before I went to school. (One would think I would be better at it than I am!) As a youngster, I was fascinated with guns, and read a lot about them. I would gaze at the guns and other equipment in that closet above our stairway. They were out of my reach, and that was probably a good thing. I am a lot more frightened of them now than when I was young, and I had a healthy respect for them then. When your children begin to carry them, your awareness of the potential for accidents increases dramatically.

I introduced the kids to guns with closely supervised target shooting, and would let them carry a single shot .22, with the bolt removed, when we took walks. It was a safe way to learn handling the weapon properly, and they did this first when they were perhaps five or six years old. All three of the kids got a real hunting bow and arrows when they were twelve or so, and if they practiced enough and shot well, I bought them a bow license and took them along hunting. Just as you may lose a few birds when you are breaking in a young dog, you will miss some chances at game while you are playing teacher for your kids and other rookies. Nonetheless, it is time well spent.

My three kids have varying interest in hunting and nature. Ben, the oldest, probably has the least. Still, he occasionally joins his siblings and me during hunting season just to experience some family time. He does like fishing quite a lot more than hunting, and I seldom fish anymore.

He has a little boy now, so I expect that I will be fishing more and Ben will be hunting more, just so that we can expose the lad to these things and all be together. Danny, the middle child, loves to fish and hunt deer. I suspect that he will become still more of an outdoorsman as he grows older. Tara is a keen observer of nature compared to other young women, and sometimes deer hunts with her brothers and me. We had some wonderful times when they were young and learning about the woods. Not long ago, she called me from her home, which has a nice pond behind it. She wanted to get my help in identifying a duck that was on the pond. She had made her own identification, and I confirmed it. I was pleased that she made the correct identification, more pleased that she cared to try.

Ben and Danny both killed large mature birds when they shot their first grouse, and I had each bird mounted. A golden retriever has since consumed Ben's mount, but Danny's bird still struts in my den. When Ben killed his bird, he stated in a matter-of-fact way, "I'm pretty young for my age to get a grouse." Tara has killed several grouse, but not gotten the mature bird that would make a good mount. I still owe her a taxidermy specimen.

During our years of target shooting and gun training, I often set up pop cans, filled with water, as targets. When you hit one of these, it makes a nice little explosion of sorts, which made the shooting more fun. Another time, I used surplus cucumbers from our garden, impaling them on sticks that I then stuck in the ground at varying distances on the target range. I was shooting with the boys that day. One of these targets was set up at perhaps forty or fifty yards from the shooter. I told the boys this was "the challenge" target.

The boys plinked away at the cucumbers, which exploded impressively when hit. Danny, who was perhaps seven or eight years old, kept begging to try to shoot at the challenge target. He was not a particularly good marksman at that point, and I wanted him to concentrate on some easier targets. I didn't want him to get frustrated shooting at targets that were too difficult. Finally, after yet another, rather whining request, I told him, "Well go ahead and try, if you hit that thing you can have the gun." We were shooting that little bolt action .22. Naturally, with his second shot, he blew the cucumber away. You never saw such an excited little boy. He jumped to his feet from the prone shooting position, hollering, "THE GUN IS MINE! THE GUN IS MINE!" And so it was, for a deal is a deal. I lost a gun that day, but I was proud of his shooting and even more proud that when he jumped up to celebrate, he first laid the gun down, pointing in a safe direction. He already had developed good habits.

Danny displayed his good habit again several years later. A buck had been wounded in the evening, and we tracked it down the next morning, finding it dead. There were several of us around the deer, and we were moving it around to begin gutting it. Somehow, one of us bumped into Danny's rifle that was leaning against a tree. There is nothing so unnerving as watching a gun fall. It landed on a log and did not go off. It did not go off because it had been unloaded and the action was open, to show that it was unloaded. Good job, son.

The kids occasionally came along when I hunted, when they them-selves were too young to actually hunt. Sometimes they sat in a deer stand or duck blind with me; other times they sat in a nearby stand while I bow hunted from another. They came along many times when I tracked down a wounded animal or went out to recover a dead one. They seemed to get a kick out it, even the gutting. Once, as I gutted out a buck with all three kids watching, Ben pointed out and identified all the internal organs for Tara as they were removed. Another time, when we returned from a duck hunt with three limits of wood ducks, Tara ran out to greet us. At the time, we were raising birds, and Tara had pet wood ducks. I wondered how she might react to a pile of dead ones. She asked if we had gotten any ducks. When I said yes, she then asked what kind. When I told her they were all wood ducks, she asked if she could see them. I was a little hesitant but opened the back door of the car and showed her the six woodies lined up on the floor of the car.

"Oh cool, Dad, can I help you gut 'em?" she exclaimed. That's my girl!

Tara has never lost her keen eye for watching critters. Her mom says she is just like her dad in that respect. When they go for a walk or four-wheeler rides together, Tara spots birds and animals and will stop to watch or approach them. When she first began deer hunting, she and I often sat together. It was quality time. Girls are definitely different in how they approach the sport, or at least my girl was.

During the bow season one year, I had been seeing a group of three does almost every time I watched my back field. They invariably entered the field on a particular trail. Tara was going to be rifle hunting that year, and she had a doe permit. I was confident we could get her a shot at this group of deer. The first evening of the season, Tara and I took a position about thirty-five yards away from, and downwind of, the spot where these deer always came into the field. We sat on the ground, using convenient trees for back rests. Tara is a southpaw and I am right-handed, so she was to my right. The spot where we expected to see the deer was slightly to her right, an ideal angle for her to train the gun.

Well, as is often the case, the deer threw us a curve. They came out at the far side of the field and off to my left. They approached us, came halfway across the field, and then stopped to feed perhaps eighty yards away. When it appeared they would come no closer, I told Tara to take the shot. She had to swing around far to her left to get the gun on them. It was an awkward shooting position, and I tried to help by leaning back and helping support the gun on my knees. When she pulled the trigger, it was a clean miss. The deer all bounced around a little, then stopped, and looked around.

"Dad... they're so stupid!" said Tara.

"Shoot again!" I hissed back.

She took another shot and the exact same thing happened.

"Dad, I can't believe they are so stupid!"

"Tara, they are not stupid. Maybe they know who is shooting at them!"

As she levered another shell into the chamber of her 30-30, the deer bounded off and disappeared behind a rise in the field. I thought they might pause at the edge of the field to look back, so I told Tara, "Let's go!" We got up and began hoofing it towards the hilltop. We moved quickly, and were hunched over to stay hidden behind the rise. As we moved along, suddenly Tara was tugging on my jacket saying, "Dad! Dad!"

"What, Tara?" I asked, a little peevishly.

"Just like in Last of the Mohicans!" she said, with a big grin, referring to the scene in the movie where an elk is run down and shot!

Well we didn't get another shot at the deer, but it was a deer encounter I will not forget.

When Tara finally got her first good chance at a deer, she passed it up because she thought the deer was sub-par. We were in a stand together while the boys made a drive. We had made this drive several times that year and each time a huge doe and a yearling had come right by this stand. Tara had not been with us on any of those occasions, but we finally got her involved in what again looked like a sure thing.

The plan worked, except the doe was not present. She was likely off

"I described my experiences outdoors and tried to convey to them how much I enjoyed those experiences."

The old-timer with son Danny.

with her big daddy and the fawn came through by itself. It stopped no more than ten yards from our stand and looked around. Tara had the gun up and had a good rest to shoot off, but she looked at the deer and declared it was just too little. I asked her in a whisper if she was sure, because it might be her only chance.

"No, Dad, it's just too little. I don't want to shoot it," she said.

I told her that was fine. I was not disappointed. She had never taken a deer, and she wanted to. Yet, she was already at the point in her evolution as a sportswoman that she declined an opportunity at what she considered a poor quality animal. You have to like that.

My nephew, Matt Tuominen, is younger than my children are. He has been my most regular young companion afield over the last several years. He loves to hunt ducks. He reminds me of his grandfather, my dad. Both baseball players and outdoorsmen, and like his grandfather was, Matt is a quiet person. His folks have told me that Matt's coaches all tell them what a coachable kid he is, and I can vouch for that. More than any young hunter I have ever had along, he listens. When I have a newcomer along, I nearly drive them crazy with all the things I am telling them. What to watch for, what to do in a certain situation, blah, blah, blah. Matt listens to it all and tries to absorb it. This is particularly rare in youngsters. He asks questions such as, "How do I know if I need to put a finishing shot into a duck?" or "If a flock comes in, does it matter which bird I shoot at?" Then he actually listens to the answers. On many occasions, after we have some action, he asks how he might have done things differently. Most people are afraid to ask questions for fear of looking foolish. Although Matt is very quiet, he overcomes that shyness because he wants to learn and wants to do it right. Already, there is little I have to tell him anymore about duck hunting. I have also put Matt on notice that he is my insurance policy. I am feebler each year, I tell him, and soon it will be he who drags the canoe into the beaver pond and sets up the decoys. I have a good hunch he will be there when I need him.

Chapter Nineteen
No Closed Season

I was wet and getting wetter, sitting on a log and waiting for the dog to come around with the rabbit he was on. The woods were soggy from one of those seeping fall rains. Somber is a word that must have been invented on a day like this with the leaves mostly fallen, skies of solid gray and weeping cold mist. Sam, who was Gary and Cheeso Zanetti's beagle, was moving a rabbit steadily in a big circle, much bigger than normal for this time of year. I was waiting on the edge of an alder swamp, in the balsam trees that ringed that thick jungle. My attention was on a mouse. A vole actually, that was foraging around a hummock of longer grass. It darted in and out of the grass, nibbling on who knows what. You don't often get to see mice for this amount of time. They may be active like this at night, but in daylight, it just doesn't happen that often. I suppose the overcast skies and the heavy cover darkened things to the point where this character thought it was night. It was a big mistake.

The weasel came out of nowhere, and was just a brown streak that hit the mouse. The resulting ball of fur bouncing around looked like something from a cartoon until they disappeared in the long grass. With a last squeal, the battle was over. The weasel appeared briefly, carrying his victim in his mouth, then disappeared. How many times a day, on every acre of wild land, do dramas like this one occur? There is always something going on out there, and I enjoy observing this stuff almost as much as I do taking part in it. It has been that way for most of my life.

When I was just a tyke, I was big into toy cowboys, Indians, and toy animals. I had sets of African critters and North American critters. I was a big reader and loved books about wild animals that described their lives and habits. I would take my little critter figures and construct habitats for them complete with hollow logs, climbing trees, creeks, and ponds. I once got a bird house kit as a gift. I hammered it together and gave it a thick coat of the gummy green paint that Dad had around, for painting everything from his wooden rowboat to the lawn furniture. I got the ladder and nailed the box up on a pole that had once been part of the structure that held up our tire swing. The swing was gone now, but the pole could still be of service. I watched with fascination as a tree swallow built its nest in the home I had provided. I was a wildlife manager, and I didn't even know it. I had made the transition from plastic models and imagination to actual work that did wildlife some good. I am sure that the good I did for this family of swallows was more than offset by the toll I took on the local bird population. I still persecuted critters with slingshot, spears, and rocks. However, I at least had done something constructive and beneficial for wildlife.

I recall lying on my back on spring days, watching the swallows soaring, swooping, and fighting over mates or nest sites. I loved exploring the tangled undergrowth along the creek in search of frogs, snakes, and tadpoles. We built box traps, caught chipmunks, and "tamed them down." We roamed the hills, pounding on hollow trees to see if a flying squirrel would glide out. Just about every spring there was an aquarium, of the homemade type, with tadpoles or minnows. Most kids did such things, but my interest in them was keener than that of the average kid.

As life goes on, a man gets busier and priorities change. Although I always tried to spend time outdoors in the off season, it was, for the most part, tied to deer scouting, dog training, or some other such activity. I got married and started a family, and the amount of free time was dwindling. Less and less did I spend time in the woods just observing things. If I had free time, I shot my bow, trained a dog, or built stands. That all changed in 1980 when we bought 67 acres of ground, surrounding the ten we already owned. My dormant dreams came suddenly to life, and I immersed myself in my study of nature and trying to improve my little corner of the world for wildlife. It has been a terrific experience.

I started it all by planning wildlife ponds, food plots, and nest boxes. It was an education, and it rekindled those nearly dead sparks inside me. I started to study the birds, the ponds, and the little critters that lived there. I thinned balsam and other common trees that were competing with my few oaks. I planted fruit and seed-bearing trees and shrubs in my yard. I monitored my nest boxes and recorded what moved in and what they produced. Soon there was volunteer work for the Department of Natural Resources, doing grouse surveys, and trips to sharptail grouse dancing grounds, just so I could see the show. The birds, mammals, reptiles, trees, and wild flowers on our land were catalogued. Bird and deer feeders were erected in the yard. It was now as if the hunting season lasted 365 days a year.

I was very excited when we got our first bluebirds in a nest box, then kestrels, saw-whet owls, and flickers. Hooded mergansers now nest every year in my wood duck boxes. One box had a clutch of these birds every year for seven years running. One spring, we had an invasion of orioles and rose-breasted grosbeaks that lasted for a week or so, and we lured the orioles to the window ledges with orange slices. My wife has even gotten into it, enjoying the hundreds of birds feeding in the yard beginning in the fall and peaking in the spring, when migrants swarm the feeders, all decked out in their breeding plumage.

A few of my hunting cronies probably think me a little soft, due to my interest in bird watching. No, that's not right. Some hunters think that, but my cronies are all pretty clued in on nature and know that you can be a naturalist and a hunter at the same time. I will admit that hunting lures me out more than anything else does, but every spring I see the sun rise, several times, from one of my photography/observation blinds. The hours that I do hunt are much more full, now that I can enjoy pretty near everything that is going on around me. Remember the beaver pond duck roost I mentioned earlier? I hunted that spot often, for several years. I could almost bet on a fast, furious shoot for just a little while every morning, then move on to other things like bird, deer, or rabbit hunting. The morning duck shoot was great, but the half-hour before it was equally thrilling. One particular morning stands out.

It was late in October and most of the ducks had left the area. I wanted to hunt the roost pond once more, before saying goodbye for the year. The moon was full and the skies clear. The canoe crackled through a skim of ice when I launched it, breaking the stillness of the chilled night air. As I reached deeper water, the ice was gone. Dead skeletons of black ash, balsam, and aspen trees reached out of the still waters of the pond and towards the sky. The brightness of the moon cast their shadows on the water. As my boat raised a gentle wake, the silvery moonlight danced off it, and silver lines emanated from my path. A beaver cruised along the far side of the pond, and it was like a black shadow, silently moving along and leaving a silver streak behind it. It was as beautiful as any scene I have ever looked upon. Corny as it sounds, I actually got goose pimples just by being there. I jammed the boat into a little grassy spot and got that morning cup of coffee poured. I sat there for forty minutes or so, waiting for shooting light.

If the sights were breathtaking, the sounds were just as impressive. As the sky brightened ever so slightly, the night sounds of barred owls and the "ker-ploonk" of slapping beaver tails were joined by the wake-up calls of the birds, including the ducks that would soon be my targets. Teal and mallards quacked, and wood ducks twittered and squealed. The brighter the sky, the noisier the ducks. I could hear the splashing of their bathing and a funny little noise that I would not have recognized except for that fact that I was raising ducks and watching them all the time. They have a habit of dipping their bill into the water and blowing their nose. It makes a distinctive, bubbling sound in the water. Many mornings I heard this happening within yards of the boat. The noise just got louder and louder until suddenly, an explosion of wings on water told me that the first flock had launched itself into the air for the morning flight. They left like this at each sunrise to go to their feeding grounds, and instantly, frost numbed fingers and toes were warm again. Eyeballs strained, looking into the semi-dark sky, trying to pick out the shadowy forms of the birds. If I spotted them in time and within range, there would be a shot or two. More often, they buzzed over, fast and low. In spite of my best efforts to be vigilant, there was a sudden, close, whistle of wings that nearly startled me out of the boat. Often, the little rockets were over me and gone before the gun reached my shoulder. This was a great hunting experience, but what made it so good was all the little preliminary stuff I could enjoy 365 days a year.

Because the great majority of my time spent afield is while hunting, most of the unusual things I have seen have been observed from a deer stand or duck blind, most often from a deer stand. I have watched mink and weasel hunting the edges of the ponds, exploring every nook and cranny they come to in their effort to find a meal. One evening, I watched a weasel hunting the dead grass along the edge of one of the ponds. He would scurry along the thin ice that had formed along the shoreline, then dart into the long grass for a while. Soon he would appear again, out on the ice. The mice that lived here knew they were in danger, for while the weasel was in the grass, a mouse scurried out and crossed an ice bridge to the island in the pond. A few minutes later, another ran out onto the ice for a short distance, and then ducked back into the grass. The weasel followed the first set of tracks part way out to the island, but then gave up. Perhaps he felt too exposed on the open ice. The last time I saw him, he was on the trail of the second mouse.

I watched a black bear sow one evening as she walked the edge of the field and passed within ten yards of my stand. Her two cubs were following her, and feeling playful. They took turns tackling each other and wrestling around. Every little while they looked ahead, saw Mom leaving them behind, and would run to catch up, only to get into another tussle as soon as they were again close to her. From that same stand I watched a skunk preparing its winter den, raking grass with its front feet as it walked backwards to the den entrance. The ball of grass beneath its belly grew and grew as it got closer to the den, and was then pulled below ground to line the hideaway where the skunk would sleep away the winter. One evening, a bobcat walked silently out of a cedar swamp and sat down directly beneath me, where I watched for deer from a permanent wooden stand. When I see such things, I smile, and sometimes get a chill up my spine. These things are going on all around us, yet almost nobody gets to see any of it. If only everyone could stop to look.

I have spent spring evenings in a hay bale blind with the video camera, hoping something worth filming would come by. If nothing did, it was great just to listen to the frogs. Ever watched a ruffed grouse drumming? Have you seen a half-dozen male sharptail dancing in circles around an aloof hen? Picked a hissing, beak-snapping, saw-whet owl off her nest to look at her babies that hatch over a two-week spell and are all different sizes? If you have ever watched body builder competitions on TV, you have seen these beefy characters bend over and put their fists knuckle to knuckle, pull their shoulders forward and grit their teeth while flexing their muscles. Did you know that the male red-winged blackbird's display, the one he shows to another male, is a very similar posture? Are you aware of how comical a gray owl looks when he plunges into the snow after prey and misses? They look around as if they are hoping nobody was watching. I once saw a white-tail buck masturbating. He didn't seem to care if anyone was watching. I also witnessed a wood duck hen being raped by a flock of drakes. I caught a part of that on video. If you feed birds and you feed during spring migration, you could see seven, eight, or more kinds of sparrows taking advantage of your handout. To most people, these are just sparrows, or "brown birds."

For the past several years, I have fought thick, wet grass, brush, and swarming mosquitoes to check out a patch of bloodroot plants in the middle of my property. I want to see them in bloom, and I have not yet succeeded. The closest I have come is to see the last few petals drooping from the stalks, the ground littered with hundreds, maybe thousands, of the fallen petals. Luck with my wild orchids is better. Three kinds of ladyslippers grow in our little reserve. There is a big patch of the yellows, and I think they are the prettiest wildflower in the state. There are three clumps of showy ladyslippers that I dug out of a road ditch to save them from the state mowers. I lugged them in a wheelbarrow into my woods to plant near my biggest pond. For years, I knew of two, yes that's right, two... purple ladyslippers. I can walk you right to them if you want to see them. Recently, we found a big patch of them that I had never seen before. Do you know what a purple, fringed orchid looks like? Why not make a point of finding out.

If you are an adult who does not understand my fascination with this stuff, nothing I write, or that anyone else writes, is likely to make you understand. If you do understand my feelings, I hope you are taking some time to explore all of the terrific stuff that surrounds you. A significant milestone on this hunter's journey was reached when I found a deep appreciation for all of these small miracles. Every square foot of wild land contains mystery and excitement. If you do not take advantage of it by enjoying it, at least occasionally, you are indeed very busy or very foolish. After all, for whom did God make this?

"Every square foot of wild land contains mystery and excitement."

A saw-whet owl peers out of its nest in a wood duck box.

Chapter Twenty
Mileposts in the Mirror

When I was in high school, people often would ask me about my life's goals and plans. I would laugh and tell them that all I wanted was a home in a rabbit swamp, with lots of dogs and lots of kids. It was said as a joke, but it was rooted in some basic truths about what I held important. I do not think I was even conscious of this truth back then. As I look at my life so far, those few dreams I had have already been realized. Cedar Valley, where my home is, is pretty much a swamp. Everybody I know from the U.P., who has hunted in Cedar Valley, gets confused when the locals talk about a hill. Yoopers know what a hill is, people from the Valley do not. In Cedar Valley, you are on a hill if your feet are dry.

I have three dogs now, and have had five or more at times. I have three kids of my own, and a kid who lived with us for a while and is now part of the gang. I call him my fake kid. In addition, there has always been a ton of cousins and pals of the kids around. Perhaps I am stretching it a little here, because I was talking about having many kids of my own. Three or four is not that many. The point is, I am happy. My wife and I get along just great. She understands my feelings about nature and hunting, and though it causes her some inconvenience now and again, she puts up with it and seldom complains. She's a looker, too! The kids grew up pretty civilized and responsible.

I live in a place where deer and bear pass through the yard and good hunting can be had just walking out the back door. My neighbors let me hunt on their land, sometimes even where nobody else is allowed. I own some acreage here that I play with, and play on, trying to make it a good place for critters to live. We had built our home on ten acres that had once been owned by my wife's grandfather, and then her father. Several years later we bought 67 additional acres. Owning land was a part of my dream that had been pushed to the back of my mind. I really didn't think I would be able to buy land for hunting, hiking, or other activities while I was young enough to enjoy it. Not thinking about it kept me from being frustrated about that situation. Yet even that dream came true in time, and it opened the door to a whole new hobby, that of habitat management.

The journey I began in the outdoors, over thirty-five years ago, continues today. People have said that I have a good memory for details such as those described on the preceding pages, which one might describe as mileposts now long behind me. Perhaps that is so. A greater gift than a good memory, however, is that of curiosity. I have always enjoyed reading. To read of something you have not experienced is an education, and a wonderful way to begin learning about something new. Better still is to then go out and try it. To experience for yourself the things you have read about completes your education and reinforces what you learned in that comfortable easy chair as you turned the pages. While I enjoy reading about things that I will never be able to do, there is a "completeness" in doing what you have read and dreamed about—a sense of accomplishment. Many of the hunting pursuits described on these pages, as well as the habitat management just mentioned, began in that comfortable chair.

Those of us who are curious always seem to have a long list of things we want to try. I have dabbled with trapping, and I may give it more attention, for it appears I may have more (or at least more flexible) time to do so. More serious trapping is a goal that is within fairly easy reach. More time may also allow me to have a hunting season similar to the one my dad had experienced while recovering from his work injury—that season he never forgot and never stopped reliving.

Other dreams are most likely out of reach. I have often toyed with the thought of trying falconry. The commitment required for becoming proficient at that ancient art, however, is likely more than I will be able to muster. If I were able to make such a commitment, to devote the amount of time that is due such an art form, I would have to put too many treasured pursuits aside. I will not give up toying with the thought, but things like ducks and dogs and wildlife watching will, I hope, never be discarded.

At this point in my life, I find it reassuring that my curiosity is still drawing me to new outdoor adventures, while I continue my long and treasured association with others. The mileposts keep coming into view even as others slip behind me. It would seem that my journey is without end. How fortunate that the route is so pleasant along the hunter's journey.

The Author

Dan Prusi was born in Ishpeming, Michigan, in 1953. He grew up in and around nearby Negaunee, and graduated from Negaunee High School in 1971, moving to Minnesota in 1972. There he married Sherilee Tuominen in 1973. The couple resides in Cedar Valley Township, near Floodwood, Minnesota, and have three grown children.

An avid outdoorsman and amateur naturalist, Dan owns and resides on a seventy-seven acre property that is managed for wildlife. After a twenty-eight year career in the manufacturing world, he has turned to writing—a life-long hobby—as a second career.

Autographed copies of this and Dan Prusi's other books:

A Hunter's Year
and
Country Boy - Adventures from an Untroubled Childhood

may be ordered directly from the author. Contact him at:
TalesFromCV@aol.com
or
Box 482, Floodwood, MN 55736-0482.